BY THE AUTHOR

Poetry

The Plain People
Between Root and Sky
The Maidenhair Tree
Ships in Bottles
Walking to Santiago
The Road to the Gunpowder House
Other Rooms (Selected Poems)
Some Letters Never Sent
On Keeping Company With Mrs Woolf
A Northumbrian Book of Hours

Translations

Euripides, The Bacchae
Euripides, The Trojan Women
Euripides, The Helen
Homer, The Bending of the Bow
Jules Supervielle, The Fable of the World
The Dream of the Rood

Criticism

Norman Nicholson
Christopher Smart
George Herbert (co-written with Natasha Curry)
Alexander Pope
Six Eighteenth-century Poets
William Cowper: a Revaluation
William Shenstone: Landscape Gardener and Poet

Topography

The Cumberland Coast

SAMUEL JOHNSON

SAMUEL JOHNSON
WRITER

NEIL CURRY

Greenwich Exchange
London

Greenwich Exchange, London

First published in Great Britain in 2022
All rights reserved

Samuel Johnson: Writer
© Neil Curry, 2022

This book is sold subject to the conditions that it shall not, by way of trade or otherwise, be lent, resold, hired out or otherwise circulated without the publisher's prior consent in any form of binding or cover other than that in which it is published and without a similar condition including this condition being imposed on the subsequent purchaser.

Printed and bound by imprintdigital.com
Cover design by December Publications
Tel: 07951511275

Greenwich Exchange Website: www.greenex.co.uk

Cataloguing in Publication Data is available
from the British Library

ISBN: 978-1-910996-49-2

CONTENTS

	Chronology	*9*
1	The Biographer	*13*
2	The Poet	*26*
3	The Dictionary Writer	*49*
4	The Essayist	*64*
5	Rasselas	*81*
6	The Scottish Tour	*97*
7	The Editor	*108*
8	The Lives of the English Poets	*118*
	Bibliography	
	Index	

CHRONOLOGY

As this study makes no attempt to add to the many biographies of Johnson which have already been written, a brief chronology is thought to be sufficient.

1709	Samuel Johnson born 18 September in Lichfield, son of a bookseller.
1717	Attends Litchfield Grammar School.
1725	Attends Stourbridge School.
1728	Goes to Pembroke College, Oxford.
1729	Leaves Oxford without a degree.
1731	Death of his father.
1732	Usher at Market Bosworth School.
1734	Translates Lobo's *Voyage to Abyssinia*, published 1735.
1735	9 July, marries Elizabeth Porter.

	Establishes school at Edial near Lichfield; David Garrick is a pupil there.
1737	Johnson and Garrick walk to London.
1737-44	Writes for *Gentleman's Magazine*.
1738	Publishes *London: A Poem*.
1740	James Boswell born in Edinburgh.
1744	Publishes *An Account of the Life of Richard Savage*.
1745	Publishes *Miscellaneous Observations on the Tragedy of Macbeth*.
1747	Publishes *A Plan for a Dictionary of the English Language*. *A Prologue* for the opening of Drury Lane Theatre under the management of David Garrick.
1749	His play *Irene* performed at Drury Lane. Publishes *The Vanity of Human Wishes*.
1750-52	Publishes *The Rambler*.
1752	Death of his wife.
1753-54	Contributes to *The Adventurer*.
1755	Receives degree of MA from Oxford. Publication of Dictionary.

1758-60	Contributes to the *Universal Visitor* as 'The Idler'.
1759	Death of his mother. Publication of *Rasselas*.
1762	Awarded £300 per annum pension.
1763	Meets Boswell.
1764	With Sir Joshua Reynolds founds The Club.
1765	Meets the Thrales. Publishes *The Dramatic Works of William Shakespeare*.
1773	Tours Scotland with Boswell.
1774	Tours Wales with the Thrales.
1775	Publishes *A Journey to the Western Islands of Scotland*.
1779	First volumes of *Lives of the English Poets* published. Death of David Garrick.
1781	Death of Mr Thrale.
1782	Falls out with Mrs Thrale. Completes *Lives of the English Poets*.
1783	Suffers a stroke, loses power of speech, but recovers.

1784	Dies 20 December, buried in Westminster Abbey.
1785	Boswell publishes *The Journal of a Tour to the Hebrides*.
1787	Publication of *The Works of Samuel Johnson* in 11 volumes with a life by Sir John Hawkins.
1791	Boswell's *Life of Samuel Johnson* published.
1795	Death of Boswell.

1
THE BIOGRAPHER

IT COULD BE SAID THAT IT was one of the most unfortunate encounters of Samuel Johnson's entire life, that Monday evening in 1763 when he set out along The Strand simply to drink a dish of tea with his friend the bookseller, Tom Davies, and found a callow young Scotsman already ensconced there, eager to meet him. It was a meeting which resulted in the writing of one of the most famous of all biographies, but what Johnson could not have foreseen was that it was a biography which would, in the general view, effectively kill him off as a writer, resurrecting him instead as a 'personality', one who would forever after be known as *Doctor* Johnson, famous predominantly for bouts of conversational jousting. It is an image which is all too clearly borne out by the *Oxford Dictionary of Quotations* in which what Boswell reports him to have *said* outnumbers at least by five times what he is recorded as having *written*. Even the few mementoes of his written work which it does carry are heavily biased towards the comic, and that even includes entries from the Dictionary. The result is that Boswell seems all too often to have managed to reduce *Ursa Major* to a performing bear.

Published in 1791, Boswell's *Life of Johnson* has been constantly and widely acclaimed, but this does not mean that it should not be open to question. It is the mine which has been worked assiduously by all Johnson's later biographers, but mines will inevitably be found to contain more dross than gold, and while it can indeed sometimes be entertaining, read in its entirety it is often dull, frequently even banal. We come across familiar and unforgettable nuggets such as young David Garrick peeping through the keyhole of the Johnson's bedroom and reporting on his 'tumultuous and awkward fondness for Mrs Johnson', but this is immediately followed, for no obvious reason, by Johnson's 'Scheme for the Classes of a Grammar School'. The temptation to skip begins early.

One of the main causes of this is the work's lack of cohesion. Boswell so venerated Johnson that he was reluctant to leave out anything. Every detail was to him equally precious, with the result that it has all the frustrating semblance of a scrapbook, with items pasted in quite haphazardly.

There is a good deal of self-veneration in it too. Boswell casts himself in a central role throughout and is at pains to let his readers know of the instant warmth of Johnson's feelings for him. 'Come to me as often as you can. I shall be glad to see you,' he is told. And again, 'There are few people to whom I take so much as you.' Now we have only Boswell's word for any of this and it is hard to square such effusiveness with the fact that after their first encounter in 1763 they did not meet again until 1766 and that during those three years Johnson wrote to him only twice and sent him only five more letters during the next six. Boswell manages to convey the impression that he was Johnson's closest friend and that they were constantly in each other's company, yet it has been calculated that over the 21 years he knew Johnson, they spent at the most 404 days together and that includes their 83-day tour of Scotland.

Boswell did not meet Johnson until 1763, by which time he had written all his major works: his two long poems, *London* and *The Vanity of Human Wishes*; the Dictionary, *Rasselas*, and every one of his essays. In recognition of this he had been awarded an annual pension of £300 (possibly as much as £50,000 today) which had relieved him of the *necessity* to write. We never forget his assertion that, 'No man, but a blockhead, ever wrote, except for money.' Therefore Boswell knew him not as a writer, but as a talker and this is what he records.

Johnson knew that Boswell would one day write his biography and seems to have been content with the idea, but there are times when we can sense his irritation. 'Sir, you have but two topics, yourself and me. I am sick of both.' And on another occasion when he realised that he was being trapped into a flyting match, the irritation turned to downright anger. 'Don't you know that it is very uncivil to *pit* two people against one another? ... I would sooner keep company with a man from whom I must guard my pockets, than with a man who contrives to bring me into dispute with somebody that he may hear it.'

Johnson himself was an accomplished biographer and his most outstanding achievement is his final work, *Lives of the English Poets*. And between 1738 and 1744, when he was in his early thirties he wrote several brief lives for the *Gentleman's Magazine*, Oliver Cromwell and Sir Francis Drake being among them, but with his *Account of the Life of Richard Savage* in 1744 he could be said to have opened up a new literary genre. It is, admittedly, something of a generalisation to argue that most earlier biographies had been black and white: saints or sinners, but for Johnson's psychological insights into Savage's achievements and failures, his vices and his virtues, there is really no precedent.

For a clearer understanding of what is to follow, some outline of Savage's life is essential, and none could better the advertisement which Johnson's publisher, James Roberts, whose speciality was scandal, inserted in the *London Evening Post*:

> An account of the life of Mr Richard Savage, son of the late Earl Rivers, who was, soon after he came into the world, bastardised by an act of Parliament, and deprived of the title and estate to which he was born, was committed by his mother, the Countess of Macclesfield, to a poor woman, to be bred up as her own son; came to the knowledge of his real mother, now alive, but abandoned by her, persecuted and condemned for murder, and against all her endeavours, pardoned; made poet laureate to Queen Caroline, became very eminent for his writings, of which many are quoted in this Work, particularly the 'Bastard' ... went into Wales, to be supported by a subscription, promoted by Mr Pope, but at last died in Prison.

Roberts had been quick to see the potential of such a Life. Bookselling itself was a rapidly expanding business, particularly the market for novels, and even more so for the new realism, especially low-life realism, such as could be seen in Defoe's *Moll Flanders*, Fielding's *Tom Jones* and *The Beggar's Opera*.

Savage's life had so much to offer: his extreme poverty, being found guilty of murder in a brothel, and finally dying in a debtors' jail. Added to which were elements which seemed to step straight from a traditional romance: a wicked (step)mother, being a child of noble birth brought up in a poor family, finding proof of his true birthright, plus the ever-popular theme of neglected genius. It was all there.

Johnson had once said that 'Nobody can write the life of a man, but those who have eat and drunk and lived in social intercourse with him', and 'social intercourse' was what he unquestionably did have with Savage: one of the clearest pointers being that extra little detail he adds to one of the closing pages, when he tells us that Savage's vanity was such that he could never, 'read his verses without stealing his eyes from the page, to discover, in the faces of his audience, how they were affected with any favourite passage.' An observation which could only have been made by someone who had been witness to it, and probably on more than one occasion. Added to this we have their famous 'night-wanderings'. Johnson tells us that:

> ... he passed the night sometimes in mean houses ... sometimes in cellars among the riot and filth of the meanest and most profligate of the rabble; and sometimes, when he had not money to support even the expenses of these receptacles, walked about the streets till he was weary and lay down in the summer upon a bulk, or in the winter, with his associates in poverty, among the ashes of a glass-house.

What Johnson omits to tell us is that he was with Savage on such nights, but Sir John Hawkins, another of Johnson's biographers, says he had told him that he was. And if there are any doubts that Johnson knew at first-hand what 'the sordid comforts of night cellars' were, his *Rambler* Essay 171 dispels them. Here, under the pretext of it being a letter from a young prostitute, we have an all-too-vivid account of what such places were like.

> If those who pass their days in Plenty and Security could visit for an Hour the dismal Receptacles to which the Prostitute retires from her nocturnal Excursions, and see the Wretches that lie crowded together, mad with Intemperance, ghastly with Famine, nauseous with Filth and noisome with Disease, it would not be easy for any degree of Abhorrence to harden them against compassion or to the Desire which they must immediately feel to rescue such numbers of Human Beings from a state so dreadful.

Theirs has often been seen as a highly unlikely friendship. Even Hawkins and Boswell agree on that, but both men are seeing Johnson as the revered, elderly gentleman they had come to know and respect. If, instead, we go back in time, the picture which presents itself to us is of a rather large, slovenly, shambling and gauche young man, his face scarred by scrofula; a failed schoolmaster who had squandered his wife's inheritance and come up from the provinces, probably with a strong midlands accent; a young man much given to bouts of melancholy and fits of convulsive twitching. It is easy to see that Johnson would have been flattered even to have been noticed, let alone befriended by this notorious and handsome sometime dandy who was what Johnson most wanted to be: a published poet. Suddenly his life was bohemian and exciting, and there had been very little in it up till then that had been at all exciting, neither his time at university, nor even his marriage. It had all been a series of failures and rejections.

But what was there in it for Savage? He had once been able to count among his friends Sir Richard Steele, Aaron Hill, and even Alexander Pope, but he was now out of favour, out of funds and out of friends. He needed an audience and an acolyte and he had found one in Johnson.

It was an unlikely friendship, yet almost inevitable. It was not simply the attraction of opposites, for despite the age-gap and many other differences, they did have a good deal in common. One thing they agreed on was that they were both unjustly neglected, that it was only poverty which held them back. As Johnson was to put it, and in capital letters in his poem *London* (published in 1738, the year of their wanderings) 'SLOW RISES WORTH, BY POVERTY DEPRESSED'. And while Savage was inveighing against the cruelty of his mother, Johnson must have thought of the strained relations he enjoyed with his. It is also possible that he was glad to be away from his wife.

There are several moments in his *Life of Savage* when Johnson could almost be describing himself. For example, when he wrote the account of Savage's outrage at his well-meaning friends having the presumption to send for a tailor to measure him for a new suit of clothes, did he not recall his own anger when as an impoverished student at Oxford he had thrown away the new boots which colleagues had generously left outside his door for him? It is hard to believe that he did not realise the extent to which he was identifying with Savage and this raises the question of how objective this biography is and whether any biography ought to be, or even can be, objective.

Johnson had strong views on the subject. 'The biographical part of literature is what I love most,' he had told Boswell and two of his *Rambler* essays are given to it. In *Rambler* 60 (Oct. 1763) his aim is to establish the difference and the disparity between biography and history. By extolling the virtues of heroes and rulers and ignoring their frailties, historians misrepresent the nature of man, he says, and urges biographers to portray those facts and feelings which are common to everyday experience. In doing so Johnson is laying down the groundwork for a new direction in biography. Histories of the downfall of kingdoms are, he argues, read with 'great tranquillity' and imperial tragedies please only by the pomp of their ornament affording us 'few lessons applicable to private life'. The word to notice here is *lessons*; the didactic element in literature is rarely far from Johnson's mind.

The distinction he is making is that between the dignity of history and the usefulness of biography, with the clear implication that what is most use is, self-evidently, of most value. Our passions, he says, will be moved only when we can recognise the pains and pleasures which are being narrated 'as our own' and can view them 'as naturally incidental to our own state of life'. It is a view summed up in his assertion that 'I have often thought that there has rarely passed a life of which a judicious and faithful narrative would not be useful.' But, while judicious and faithful, a biography will also, he implies, be 'an act of the imagination', even going so far as to use the word 'deception': 'so that we feel, while the deception lasts, whatever emotions would be excited by the same good or evil happening to ourselves'. He adds a warning on this score: that 'If the biographer write from personal knowledge ... there is danger lest his interest, his fear, his gratitude ... tempt him to conceal, if not to invent.' Nothing can better personal knowledge, however, as he insists in a memorable and incontrovertible dictum, ' ... more knowledge may be gained of a man's real character by a short conversation with one of his servants than from a formal and standard narrative, beginning with his pedigree and ending with his funeral.'

Johnson's *Life of Savage* had been written some twelve years before the *Rambler* essay and he had perhaps forgotten his own practices, for one cannot help wondering how judicious and faithful the opening pages of it are, as the narrative we are given would seem to be exactly as he would have heard it from Savage himself – hardly an unbiased narrator.

The claims being made by Savage were, at the very least, contentious and one might have expected Johnson to weigh up the evidence and seek to justify them in some way. Instead, he not only presents the claims as established facts, he goes further, condemning and castigating Savage's mother at every turn. From the outset we are told that she 'took every opportunity of aggravating his misfortunes, and obstructing his resources, and with an implacable and restless cruelty [would] continue to persecute him from the first hour of his life to the last'. She is almost a pantomime villain. It is a wonderful story he is telling, told with such gusto and with some splendid asides, such as when Savage is 'reduced to the utmost miseries of want' and having 'no profession, became an author'.

When we come to the murder and Savage's trial, Johnson

combines all the skills of a novelist with those of an accomplished and learned counsel for the defence. It begins in a very low-key and matter-of-fact way as though to assure us that we are about to have a totally objective account. 'On the 20th of November 1727 Mr Richard Savage came from Richmond, where he then lodged, that he might pursue his studies with less interruption.' But of course these few bland words have a motive behind them and lead us to believe that Mr Savage is a sober, respectable and studious citizen. He *accidentally* meets two *gentlemen* and they *happened unluckily* to go into a coffee-house. Johnson refrains at this point from telling us that it was a brothel or that in the brawl they got into Savage murdered someone. Instead, 'one Mr James Sinclair was killed.'

There follows a narrative tour de force in which we are given the judge's contemptuous and sarcastic summing-up, but not in his words, nor in Johnson's, but 'as Mr Savage used to relate it, with this eloquent harangue'. It was evidently one of Savage's party-pieces, richly comic, no doubt performed in bar after bar and rewarded with drinks.

He was nevertheless found guilty of murder and sentenced to death. A plea was made for a royal pardon, but his mother used her influence with the Queen 'in a manner so outrageous and implacable' that it was turned down. Thus had Savage perished by the evidence of 'a bawd, a strumpet and his mother, had not justice and compassion procured him an advocate of rank too great to be rejected.' This was the Countess of Hertford, patron of James Thomson, supporter of the peasant poet Stephen Duck and a friend to literature and poets in general. She it was who won him a reprieve.

While he was in jail a pamphlet known as *The Old Bailey Pamphlet* had been published to support the mercy plea. In its appeal for sympathy it made public the full story of Savage's birth, persuading readers to believe that it was Lady Macclesfield's cruel and unnatural treatment of her son that had led him into this awful plight. It was a brilliant advertising ploy and guaranteed to succeed whether Savage was hanged or reprieved. It made him famous and within weeks of his freedom (not years as Johnson says) he had published his poem *The Bastard*. With such an in-your-face title it was an instant success and went through five editions in as many months.

Savage now had fame and readers and he also had wealth due to Lady Macclesfield's nephew, Lord Tyrconnel, who, as Boswell tells us, 'received him into his family, treated him as his equal and engaged to allow him a pension of two hundred pounds a year.' A generosity which suggests Lord Tyrconnel must have believed his claims and recognised the trouble he could cause.

This was the high point of Savage's life, but it did not last. As Johnson observed, 'he had not often a friend long, without obliging him to become a stranger.' Certainly his abuse of Lord Tyrconnel's generosity was outrageous. He treated the house as his own, ordered the servants about, and invited in all his friends. He even sold some of his host's collection of valuable books. Inevitably, he was shown the door and the pension stopped. It was, in Johnson's words, 'a precipitation from plenty to indigence.' His sometime friends all left him, showing 'how much is added to the lustre of genius by the ornaments of wealth.'

It was at this point that he and Johnson met and their night-wanderings began, and it is at this point that a change occurs in the book. Previously Johnson had shown great sympathy for all that had been *done* to Savage, but now he begins to show far less for what Savage *does*. We recall the emphasis he had put in his *Rambler* essay on the usefulness of biography and we see the moral element being brought into focus. We are also now being encouraged to learn from what Savage never did: he never once blamed himself for any of the misfortunes which befell him.

> By imputing none of his miseries to himself, he continued to act upon the same principles. and to follow the same path, was never made wiser by his sufferings, nor preserved by one misfortune from falling into another.

He had always, Johnson tells us, closed his eyes to 'what he never wished to see, his real self.'

It is interesting that while the first half of the *Life of Savage* seems to run, as has been said, parallel with the low-life realism of the eighteenth-century novel, so this second half reflects the psychological investigations into emotions and feelings we encounter in Samuel Richardson's heart-searching novels, *Pamela* and *Clarissa*. Furthermore, his inclination to believe that many psychological problems may have their origin in the events of childhood brings him close to the twenty-first century.

Eventually everyone grew weary of Savage and it was proposed to gather a subscription together, enough to pack him off to Wales, where he soon fell out with those who helped him, drank too much and died in a debtors' jail. While rightly severe on him, Johnson never ceases to pity him and there is little, even in Dickens, to exceed the pathos of Savage's final moments as he records them:

The last time that the keeper saw him was on 31 July, 1743, when Savage, seeing him at his bedside, said with an uncommon earnestness, 'I have something to say to you, sir', but after a pause, moved his hand in a melancholy manner; and, finding himself unable to recollect what he was going to communicate, said, ''tis gone!' The keeper soon after left him and the next morning he died.

Johnson's partiality for the man led him to overestimate him as a poet and including his Life among the *Lives of the English Poets* was a mistake. In sheer bulk it is the equal of those on Milton, Dryden and Pope, which Savage certainly was not.

Nevertheless, the *Life of Savage* established Johnson's reputation and led, within two years, to a meeting of a consortium of booksellers at which it was agreed that he was the man to be invited to compile a dictionary – a dictionary which was to become *the* dictionary, *Johnson's Dictionary*.

2
THE POET

IN MAY 1738 JOHNSON PUBLISHED HIS extended poem *London*, an imitation of Juvenal's 'Third Satire'. His familiarity with Juvenal would have been such that he, unlike us, would have realised how close the situation of it was to that of his friend Richard Savage leaving London to live in Wales, but Dryden's Preface to his verse translation of the same satire makes the connection clear:

> Umbritius the friend of Juvenal and himself a poet, is leaving Rome, and retiring to Cumae. Our author accompanies him out of town. Before they take leave of each other, Umbritius tells his friend the reasons which oblige him to lead a private life, in an obscure place. He complains that an honest man cannot get his bread in Rome. That none but flatterers make their fortune there.

In Johnson's imitation the friend goes under the name of Thales.

There is, however, an important and fundamental difference between Dryden and Johnson. Dryden offers his readers a translation which follows the Latin closely, preserving the Roman names, and the situations it recounts remain those prevalent in Juvenal's Rome; whereas Johnson selects and adapts those aspects of the poem that serve his own purpose, which is to present his views on contemporary London. His poem is not a translation but an *imitation*, a new genre which had made its appearance and reached its peak in Pope's masterly *Imitations of Horace*.

The opening lines of *London* keep close to the original as though Johnson felt the need to make it clear to his readers which of Juvenal's Satires was being imitated. Very few today have such knowledge of Latin, so it is worthwhile, even if only for a short space, to put Johnson's lines against those of a formal translation. For example, Peter Green's translation of the poem's closing lines read:

> There are many other arguments I could adduce: but the sun
> Slants down, my cattle are lowing, I must be on my way –
> The muleteer has been signalling me with his whip
> For some while now. So, goodbye and don't forget me –
> Whenever you go back home for a break from the city, invite
> Me over too, to share your fields and coverts,
> Your country festivals. I'll put on my thickest boots
> And make the trip to those chilly uplands – and listen
> To your *satires*, if I am worthy of that honour.

Whereas Johnson's conclusion reads:

> Much could I add, – but see the Boat at hand,
> The tide retiring calls me from the Land.
> Farewell! – When Youth and Health and Fortune spent
> Thou fly'st for Refuge to the Wilds of Kent,
> And tired like me with Follies and with Crime,

> In angry Numbers warn'st succeeding Times;
> Then shall thy Friend, nor thou refuse his Aid,
> Still Foe to Vice, forsake his Cambrian Shade;
> In Virtue's cause once more exert his Rage,
> Thy Satire point, and animate thy Page.

The geographical differences are immediately obvious; this is not Juvenal's Rome, it is Johnson's England and Thales/Savage is sailing from Greenwich to Wales. Less obvious, but more significant, is the greater emphasis there is on moral issues. The poet left behind seems almost certain to find himself writing angry satires against the follies and crimes he sees around him, in which case Thales offers to come back to help him 'in Virtue's cause'. Juvenal's satire was largely directed against the social, economic and cultural ills of Rome, whereas Johnson is more concerned with the political corruption he saw in Walpole's Whig government and so it is worth noting that the original Thales was a Greek philosopher famous not only for his moral wisdom, but for his passionate opposition to tyranny.

Johnson (I will call the first speaker that for convenience sake) is not surprised that Thales should want to leave a city where:

> ... Malice, Rapine, Accident conspire,
> And now a Rabble rages, now a Fire.
> Their Ambush here relentless Ruffians lay,
> And here the fell Attorney prowls for prey;
> Here falling Houses thunder on your Head
> And here a female Atheist talks you dead.
>
> (13-18)

The physical squalor and danger equate with the city's moral degeneracy; the last two lines suggesting that neither body nor soul is safe.

Such generalised complaints could apply equally to London or to Rome, but specific contemporary references soon become evident. Walpole's opponents had been urging him to go to war with Spain which was claiming a right to search English trading vessels and Johnson looks back to a time when, in contrast, the British navy was 'The Guard of Commerce and the Dread of Spain'. This was of course:

> Ere masquerades debauch'd, Excise oppress'd
> Or English Honour grew a standing Jest.
>
> (29-30)

'Excise' is the word which would have stood out here; political controversy raged around it and in his Dictionary he would later define it as, 'A hateful tax levied upon commodities and adjudged not by the common judges of property, but wretches hired by those to whom the excise is paid.'

At this point the poem becomes a monologue spoken by Thales. Since worth and learning go unrewarded in the face of 'Vice and Gain', he asks:

> Grant me, kind Heaven, to find some happier Place,
> Where Honesty and Sense are no Disgrace.
>
> (43-44)

He does not regret his decision to leave and declares:

> Here let those reign, whom Pensions can incite
> To vote a Patriot black, a Courtier white.
>
> (51-52)

And again we have a word which is charged with contemporary relevance: a *Pension* Johnson defined (before receiving his own) as 'In England it is generally understood to mean pay given to a state hireling for treason to his country'.

His list of his country's ills continues:

> Let such raise Palaces, and Manors buy,
> Collect a tax or farm a Lottery.
> With warbling Eunuchs fill a licens'd Stage,
> And lull to Servitude a thoughtless Age.
>
> (57-60)

Then, as now, the government raised lotteries to fund public works, even the building of Westminster Bridge. Walpole's Licensing Act of 1737 was intended to ensure that no plays critical of himself and his government could be performed. Instead they favoured Italian operas which Johnson viewed with contempt.

The moral position in such passages is clear, but there are also moments of a more personal nature. Frustration and disappointment were feelings which Johnson and Savage shared and we can sense that Johnson's voice is to be heard alongside Thales' when he says he is likely to 'Live unregarded, unlamented die.' (l. 82)

The social ills of Rome were largely what concerned Juvenal in his Third Satire and he put the blame squarely on the influx of Greeks. Taking a lead from this, Johnson directs his scorn towards the French. Xenophobia and racism, it seems, have a long history.

> Their Air, their Dress, their Politics import;
> Obsequious, artful, voluble and gay,

On Britain's fond Credulity they prey.
No gainful Trade their industry can 'scape,
They sing, they dance, clean Shoes or cure a clap.

(110-114)

The influence of France had been dominant in the arts and fashion ever since King Charles returned from exile in France and had been regularly condemned and ridiculed.

From attacks on the French, Johnson moves to a theme closer to home: poverty. Johnson was always sensitive about his poverty, conscious of how it had held him back and it is significant that the one line in the poem which is entirely written in capitals reads:

SLOW RISES WORTH, BY POVERTY DEPRESSED.

(177)

London is built up on a series of contrasts: the virtues of the country and the corruption of the city; the heroic past and the decadent present; the honesty and independence of the British and the duplicity and servility of the French. The balance of Johnson's couplets is, of course, the ideal medium for contrasts of this nature.

From poverty the poem moves on to a comparison of the country and the city. Country life, with which Johnson was not familiar, is presented in rather generalised terms:

There ev'ry Bush with Nature's music rings,
There ev'ry Breeze bears Health upon its wings.

(220-221)

But the hazards of the city are given to us in some of the most vivid lines in the poem:

> Prepare for Death, if here at night you roam,
> And sign your Will before you sup from home,
> Some fiery Fop, with new commission vain,
> Who sleeps on Brambles till he kills his Man,
> Some frolic Drunkard, reeling from a Feast,
> Provokes a Broil, and stabs you in the chest.

This stabbing comes very close to Richard Savage's drunken brawl, but it is there in Juvenal and to have avoided it might have equally raised eyebrows among those in the know.

The success of the poem shows how quickly Johnson's contemporary readers recognised and responded to his portrayal of the issues, but what of today's readers? Is there anything we recognise in his themes?

> ... that England is no longer a great military power
> ... the collapse of traditional values
> ... government corruption
> ... the centralisation of power
> ... the influence of immigration
> ... inequality of wealth and justice
> ... rise of street crime, especially knife crime
> ... exorbitant rents in the capital
> ... worsening relationship with other European states
>
> Plus ça change ...

It had been the attraction of the theatre which had persuaded Johnson to leave his birthplace, Lichfield, and head for London, but the play, *Irene*, on which he had set his hopes was flatly rejected everywhere. In contrast, his young companion, David Garrick, who had been a pupil in one of Johnson's several attempts to found a school, met with almost instant success as an actor and by 1747 he was able to lay out the sum of £8,000 to take over the management of Drury Lane Theatre himself and for the opening night he invited Johnson to write a 'Prologue'.

The 'Prologue' opens with a brief history of the English theatre from the time of Shakespeare to Johnson's own day. 'Immortal' Shakespeare is praised for combining imagination, passion and truth to nature. He is followed by Ben Jonson, who in contrast is 'mortal born' and shows only 'laborious Art'. Next come the playwrights of the Restoration, who are condemned for their lack of morality.

> Themselves they studied. As they felt, they writ,
> Intrigue was Plot, Obscenity was Wit.
> Vice always found a sympathetic Friend;
> They pleased their Age and did not seek to mend.

The neo-classical writers who followed them are seen as 'Crush'd by Rules' and 'frigid', whereas the contemporary theatre is in contrast dismissed as 'Exulting Folly ... Pantomime and Song'.

The voice we now hear is that of the theatre manager himself complaining:

> Hard is his Lot, that here by Fortune plac'd
> Must watch the wild Vicissitudes of Fate.

And in conclusion he lays the responsibility for change on the audience before him.

> 'Tis yours this Night to bid the Reign commence
> Of rescu'd Nature, and reviving Sense,

> To change the Charms of Sound, the Pomp of Show
> To useful Mirth, and salutary Woe,
> Bid scenic Virtue form the rising Age,
> And Truth diffuse her Radiance from the Stage.

As ever the stress is on Virtue and Truth. It is a bold piece of writing and one cannot help thinking that Garrick felt he owed Johnson something in return, but it was another two years before he agreed to stage Johnson's *Mahomet and Irene*, as he at first insisted on calling it.

In brief, the play tells how at the fall of Constantinople in 1453, two beautiful Greek maidens, Irene and Aspasia, were captured by the Turks. The Sultan fell in love with Irene, but to become his queen she would have to renounce her religion. This is the moral conflict of the play. Aspasia is the voice of reason and virtue, struggling to prevent such a betrayal of all that was Christian. In a sub-plot, Mahomet's deputy, fearing that Irene is causing Mahomet to neglect his rule, plots to have her assassinated. Mahomet, believing, bizarrely, Irene to be involved in a plot to assassinate him, has her murdered, but learning too late of her innocence becomes distraught and orders the murderers to be put to death. It is a very operatic plot.

As a play, *Irene* fails in so many ways. Johnson's poor hearing and eyesight meant that he rarely ever went to the theatre and this may be why he fails to recognise that there must be something for the audience to *watch*. His *Dictionary* definition of 'Drama' highlights the problem: 'a poem accommodated to action'. Garrick devised exotic scenery and provided his actors with sumptuous costumes, but nothing ever *happens*. People walk on, pontificate and walk off. There is hardly any differentiation in character and all the protagonists sound the same: like the author of the essays in *The Rambler*.

Irene also suffers from a lack of genuine emotion. Abdulla, a Turkish officer, claims to be violently in love with Aspasia, whom he has just briefly caught sight of, which makes his passionate protestations only succeed in sounding very silly, while Irene herself never shows the slightest love for Mahomet whom she marries, and this is remarkable as her religious 'debate' is the only real interest the play has.

From the outset the Turks are doubtful whether Irene will agree to 'receive the Faith of Mecca', and it is surprising that Irene ever considers it at all after the Sultan tells her she need not bother herself about the fate of her immortal soul as she hasn't got one and will never go to heaven no matter what:

> For your inferior Natures
> Form'd to delight, and happy by delighting
> Heav'n has reserv'd no future Paradise.

She argues her case eloquently but the argument is clearly Johnson's not hers, and her apostasy follows from the worst of reasons: the plot demands it and not from anything in the psychology of the character.

When she is finally murdered at the Sultan's command, it looks as though she has been dealt her just deserts for giving up her religion to save her life and to gain wealth and power. We feel no pity for her. Hers is not a tragedy despite what it says on the title page of the printed version.

Johnson had certainly finished a first draft of the play some fifteen years previously and when performed it must have seemed very old-fashioned. Nevertheless, it can be considered to have been something of a success in that it ran for a total of nine nights. On its first night Johnson dressed himself up for the part, incongruously wearing a scarlet waistcoat and a gold-laced hat.

Gloomy and melancholic though he sometimes was, Johnson could at times be the most sociable of men, renowned not only for the cut and thrust of his conversation, but also for the satirical wit of his extempore poetry. Poor Thomas Percy, he of the *Reliques of Ancient English Poetry*, praised for the simplicity of one of his own ballads, had to listen as Johnson demonstrated his contempt for the mechanical and vacuous jog-trot of it by turning to his hostess Frances Reynolds, and asking her:

> I therefore pray thee Renny dear,
> That thou will give to me
> With cream and sugar soften'd well
> Another cup of tea.
>
> Nor fear that I, my gentle maid,
> Shall long detain the cup,
> When once unto the bottom I
> Have drunk the liquor up.
>
> Yet hear alas! this mournful truth,
> Nor hear it with a frown –
> Thou canst not make the tea so fast
> As I can gulp it down.

There was more apparently, but even when he was stopped he declared, 'Poetry! I could speak such Poetry extempore for seven years together if I could find Hearers dull enough to attend to me.'

Extempore poetry could also be turned into a party game and according to Fanny Burney, she and Johnson and Mrs Thrale took turns in composing this Elegy.

> Here's a Woman of the Town,
> Lies dead as any Nail!
> She was once of high Renown –
> And so here begins my Tale.
>
> She was once as Cherry plump
> Red her Cheek as Cath'rine Pear;
> Toss'd her nose and shook her Rump,
> Till she made the Neighbours stare.
>
> There she soon became a Jilt,
> Rambling often to and fro'
> All her Life was naught but Guilt
> Till Purse and Carcase both were low.
>
> But there came a Country Squire.
> He was a seducing Pug!
> Took her from her Friends and Sire,
> To his own House her did lug.
>
> Black her Eye with many a Blow,
> Hot her breath with many a Dram,
> Now she lies exceeding low,
> As quiet as a Lamb.

The deliberate awfulness of some of the lines – especially 'To his own House her did lug' is quite brilliant, as is the audacity of 'Toss'd her Nose and shook her Rump'.

But 1748, the year when his other lengthy and ambitious poem,

The Vanity of Human Wishes was written, was not a happy time for Johnson. He was beginning to realise that his original scheme for his Dictionary was not going to work and that he would have to adopt a whole new approach. On top of this, his wife's health was starting to fail and this was not helped by the opiates she was taking for imagined ailments, nor by her heavy drinking. The 'noisome air' of Gough Square where Johnson and his amanuenses were working on the Dictionary was also upsetting her and she moved to 'a small house beyond the church' in the village of Hampstead, so that Johnson had to keep travelling from one house to the other. Considering all this it becomes clear why he chose Juvenal's Tenth Satire to work on.

It is hard to rid one's mind of those bleak words which Johnson penned in the opening paragraph of his *Life of Savage*: 'the general lot of mankind is misery'. And it is not an isolated sentiment but one which we find in so many different areas of his work. In his novel *Rasselas* the poet Imlac concludes that 'Human life is everywhere a state in which much is to "be endured and little to be enjoyed."' And in *Rambler* 120 we read, 'When we take the most distant prospect of life, what does it present us but a chaos of unhappiness, a confused and tremulous scene of labour and contest, disappointment and defeat' – words which stand out as being remarkably close to the 'extensive view' we are presented with at the start of *The Vanity of Human Wishes*:

> Let Observation with extensive View
> Survey Mankind from China to Peru;
> Remark each anxious Toil, each eager Strife,
> And watch the busy Scenes of crowded Life.
>
> (1-4)

But we need to remember that the title of the poem is *The Vanity of Human WISHES* not *The Vanity of Human LIFE*.

What determines our wishes, Johnson asserts, are Hope and Fear. Nowadays we no longer know how to read such capitalised abstractions, so we need to pause and try to flesh them out so as to see what Johnson means by them and when we do we realise how succinct (though arguably rather too succinct) he is being. We always *Hope* that something nice might happen to us, while at the same time *Fear* that something horrid might. Those two words can indeed be seen as driving and encompassing all our wishes, but of course there are many different kinds of nice things and even more which are horrid and it is this fact which Johnson investigates in what follows and which can be seen as having the shape and design of a sermon: statements elucidated by exempla.

The examples vary between the generalised and the specific. Wealth – something we all feel we could do with more of – comes first and is approached through the generalised terms of, 'How much more safe the Vassal than the Lord'. That no one is likely to waste his time robbing a poor man is expressed in a delightful couplet with a rhythm of carefree contentment and happiness:

> The needy Traveller, serene and gay,
> Walks the wild Heath, and sings his Toil away.
>
> (37-38)

But give him some money, Johnson says, and he'll soon have to start worrying:

> Now fears in dire Vicissitude invade,
> The rustling Brake alarms, and quiv'ring Shade.
>
> (41-42)

Fame, as it is enjoyed by noble politicians, is seen to be as ephemeral as a firework:

> They mount, they shine, evaporate and fall
>
> (76)

The vanity of pride, ambition and power are depicted in the fall of Cardinal Wolsey. At the height of his power his smile alone could secure the safety of a courtier, but 'At length his sov'reign frowns' and Wolsey promptly falls out of favour. 'Grief aids disease', and he dies, friendless, in a monastery. It is certainly a brief and vivid account of the story, but the balanced clauses and the thumping regularity of the caesura do not make for easy reading.

> At once is lost the Pride of awful State
> The golden Canopy, the glitt'ring Plate,
> The regal Palace, the luxurious Board,
> The liv'ried Army, and the menial Lord,
> With Age, with Cares, with Maladies oppresss'd,
> He seeks the Refuge of Monastic Rest.
>
> (113-118)

From politics we move to academia and the picture of a young student burning with ambition to be recognised for his intellectual ability – perhaps a memory of Johnson's own feelings about his failure at Oxford.

> When first the College Rolls receive his Name,
> The young Enthusiast quits his Ease for Fame;
> Through all his Veins the Fever of Renown
> Burns from the strong Contagion of the Gown.
>
> (135-138)

Fever points to such ambition as being a sickness, and *contagion* recalls the poisoned shirt which brought an end to Heracles.

In contrast we now leave the scholar in his carrel and find ourselves on a battlefield with a king: the reckless, vainglorious, over-reaching Charles XII of Sweden whose ambition was that, 'all be Mine beneath the Polar Sky', but who met an inglorious end at the calamitous siege of Frederikshald, shot by a stray bullet fired, it is believed, by one of his own men. The double irony is that while this had taken place as recently as 1718 and would still have been fresh in the minds of many of the poem's first readers, Charles XII now exists only in the footnotes of history and has not even, as Johnson predicted:

> left the name at which the world grew pale
> To point a moral, or adorn a tale.
>
> (221-222)

Everything now changes and we are presented with the various miseries which can be expected in the long life so many wish for. 'Life protracted is protracted woe', we are told, and depressing proofs occupy the next 63 lines. Our eyesight will fail so we will not be able to see the beauty of the passing seasons; we will lose our sense of taste and go deaf to the 'soothing sounds' of music. We will bore our friends and relations by repeating over and over again the same old tales. A detailed list of the 'unnumbered maladies' which are waiting for us, we are mercifully spared and Johnson does go so far as grant that some of us will 'glide in modest Innocence away', but even this concession is followed by a 'Yet' and there is no happiness in such an end as our friends and family will be falling ill and dying all around us. Finally, what sort of end is in store for those whose lives might seem to have been successful?

> In Life's last Scene what Prodigies surprise,
> Fears of the Brave, and Follies of the Wise?
> From *Marlb'rough's* Eyes, the Streams of Dotage flow
> And *Swift* expires a Driv'ler and a Show.
>
> (317-318)

Johnson might well have also had Swift's deathless Struldbrugs in mind here, but the final effect is not what he intended. Far from being convinced that life is like this, such an accumulation of gloom rather makes us feel pity for the man for whom it appears so.

But the catalogue of misery is still not at an end. Beauty? That will not last.

> Here Beauty falls betray'd, despis'd, distress'd,
> And hissing Infamy proclaims the rest.
>
> (341-342)

At this point the reader can see that fewer than 30 lines remain to bring this to a satisfactory conclusion. Johnson's poem has contained a lot of negatives and they cannot be dismissed or reversed quite so quickly. The opening proposition which declared that Hope and Fear were snares now seems to have been forgotten and we are being invited to ask ourselves, 'Where then shall Hope and Fear their Objects find?'

Juvenal's Tenth Satire is of course not a religious poem and the stoicism which he advocates at its close is not something which could be acceptable to a Church of England Christian and Johnson rejects it.

> Must dull Suspense corrupt the stagnant Mind?
> Must helpless Man in Ignorance sedate,
> Roll darkling down the Torrent of his Fate?
> Must no Dislike alarm, no Wishes rise,
> No Cries attempt the Mercies of the Skies?
>
> (345-348)

But we are still left waiting and eventually all he has to offer is that only religion provides a lasting source of hope, and the fact that happiness is not to be achieved here on earth is held to imply the existence of a spiritual realm in which it will be. He tells us we are wasting our time praying for material blessings. We must leave it all to God. Love and faith are what will save us and the closing couplet reads:

> With these celestial Wisdom calms the Mind,
> And makes the Happiness she does not find.
>
> (367-368)

It is not easy to grasp what he really means by this, nor the lines leading up to it, which while they have the appearance of an intellectual justification, are suggestive but hardly persuasive.

The Vanity of Human Wishes does not make for enjoyable reading. Its lack of continuity – admittedly a consequence of Juvenal's original – does not help. Unlike *London*, it was not reprinted and was never popular. It is resolutely Augustan and seems backward-looking in its use of couplets. A new movement was beginning to be felt in poetry, a movement which favoured the lyric rather than the couplet, the imaginative over the didactic. Romanticism was something he did not see coming and if he had, he would have done all he could to stop it.

Anyone who has just read right through to the end of *The Vanity of Human Wishes* could be forgiven for refusing to believe that Johnson had also written a poem about his father teaching him to swim when he was a little boy living in Lichfield. He did, but *mirabile dictu*, it is in Latin. It begins:

> Errat adhuc vitreus per prata virentia rivus,
> Quo toties lavi membra tenalla puer;
> Hic delusa rudi frustrabar brachia motu,
> Dum docuit blanda voce nature pater.

> Through green fields that glassy stream
> Still wanders, where, once in, I would, as a boy,
> Flail my arms about, hopelessly inept, while my
> Father stood quietly by encouraging me to swim.

My free version may be inept, but it shows what Johnson was saying and it is surprisingly personal and touching and quite unlike anything he had ever written in English. And it is followed by an equally surprising description of the place itself: overhanging branches had made it a secret hiding place where the waters were dark even in bright daylight. But, he tells us, 'cruel axes' have since cut these trees down and his bathing place is now wide open and can be seen by anyone. An image of lost innocence and a sad reflection which predates Cowper's lyric 'The Poplar Field' by several years. But not something he would have written in English. Emotion of that nature had, seemingly, to be covered by a veil.

Also in Latin is Johnson's 'Know Yourself' sub-titled 'After Enlarging and Correcting the English Dictionary'. It was 1772 and he had just completed the revisions for the Fourth Edition.

He was exhausted and tells us so, but not immediately. Autobiography was not yet an accepted literary genre either, and so Johnson again hides his feelings, first behind Latin and then by telling us – as though by way of justification – how the Renaissance polymath Scaliger (1540-1609) had felt when he finished *his* dictionary. It is not until Johnson is almost half way through his poem that he confesses his own feelings, feelings which his friend the playwright Arthur Murray translated:

> The listless will succeeds, that worse disease,
> The rack of indolence, the sluggish ease.
> Care grown on care, and o'er my aching brain
> Black Melancholy pours her morbid train.
> No kind relief, no lenitive at hand.
> I seek at midnight clubs the social band;
> But midnight clubs, where wit with noise conspires,
> Delight no more; I seek my lonely bed,
> And call on Sleep to soothe my languid head.
> But Sleep from these sad lids flies far away;
> I mourn all night, and dread the coming Day

Johnson must have been aware of his achievement but the feeling of anti-climax is understandable. That such 'Confessional Poetry' was possible, but had to be veiled in Latin shows us how little we really understand the eighteenth-century mind.

As years went by, some of the predictions he had made about old age in *The Vanity of Human Wishes* began to come true. His health was failing; he suffered from bowel problems, rheumatism and gout, and added to his melancholia was a fear of dying and a dread of going mad. But he never ceased to care for the miscellaneous collection of needy souls he was giving houseroom. A longstanding 'guest' was Robert Levet, an unlicensed doctor with no professional training, who spent his life walking daily through the streets of the city caring for those more destitute than himself. Boswell had no time for him and could not understand Johnson's 'fanciful estimate of his moderate abilities', but did add, 'I have heard him say that he should not be satisfied, though attended by all the College of Physicians, unless he had Mr Levet with him.' Sullen, not always sober, uncouth, wizened and scarred by smallpox, Levet seemed grotesque to some of Johnson's friends. Hawkins said he 'disgusted the rich and terrified the poor.' But Johnson would not have a word said against him and when Levet died in 1782 he wrote an elegy for him which was published in *The Gentleman's Magazine*:

> Condemn'd to hope's delusive mine,
> As on we toil from day to day,
> By sudden blasts, or slow decline,
> Our social comforts drop away.

This opening stanza with its pointer to the delusive nature of hope is in tune with the sentiments of *The Vanity of Human Wishes* and raises the poem above a concern with a single individual. We are all in the same predicament – the grim image he presents us with is one of slaves condemned to toiling in a mine and it is an image which is skilfully continued: we notice *caverns*, *chains* and *freed* in the stanzas which follow. But as the poem develops the tone of these quatrains becomes more colloquial than that of the heroic couplet he had used in *Vanity*, more relaxed and personal, more Horatian.

Unrefined Levet certainly was, but he was also 'Of ev'ry friendless name the friend' and there is no hint of condescension when Johnson describes his work as a physician to the poor:

> When fainting nature call'd for aid,
> And hov'ring death prepar'd the blow,
> His vig'rous remedy display'd
> The power of art without the show.
>
> In misery's darkest caverns known,
> His useful care was ever nigh,
> Where hopeless anguish pour'd his groan,
> And lonely want retir'd to die.
>
> No summons mock'd by chill delay,
> No petty gain disdain'd by pride,
> The modest wants of ev'ry day
> The toil of ev'ry day supplied.
>
> (13-24)

We learn so much in these compact stanzas, and not only about Robert Levet, but about the professional physicians of his day, too proud to treat the poor, demonstrating their self-importance by making their patients wait and then their treatment being more for show than usefulness – accusations which still strike a chord. Levet on the other hand, went into the darkest caverns where the lonely and the destitute 'retir'd to die' and when we read these lines we remember Johnson's account in *Rambler* 171 of the squalor in which the prostitutes lived. And Levet was not doing this for the money. As we are told, he was sometimes paid in kind with whatever the poor had, and unfortunately that was sometimes gin.

In stanza seven Johnson pays him the highest praise in what is a reference to the Parable of the Talents:

> His virtues walked their narrow round,
> Nor made a pause, nor left a void;
> And sure th'Eternal Master found
> The single talent well employ'd.

Johnson, as Boswell tells us, would often blame himself for indolence and wasting his own talents. 'The solemn text "of him to whom much is given, much will be required", seems to have been ever present in his mind.'

Levet's own health held up to the end and he died of a heart attack at the age of 77.

> The busy day, the peaceful night,
> Unfelt, uncounted, glided by;
> His frame was firm, his powers were bright,
> Tho' now his eightieth year was nigh.

> Then with no throbbing, fiery pain,
> Nor cold gradation of decay,
> Death broke at once the vital chain,
> And freed his soul the nearest way.

In one of his less perceptive moments Johnson was to criticise Milton's *Lycidas* for a lack of sincerity, having 'no effusion of real passion', but behind the grave seriousness of this elegy we can sense a real appreciation of the man and real personal grief at his loss.

3

THE DICTIONARY-WRITER

IN THE EARLY YEARS OF THE seventeenth century there was an exuberance and extravagance in the language of both poetry and prose, an inventiveness in the syntax, words packed with layers of meaning and metaphors of a rich complexity. It is there in John Donne's poems and in his sermons. When the reaction against such complexity came – as it was sure to do – it came from several directions, but famously from the newly-formed scientific organisation The Royal Society, which urged its members to return to the 'purity and shortness' of language, 'bringing all things as near a mathematical plainness as they can.' A committee was set up to foster these reforms and one member, the poet Dryden, complained that 'we have not so much as a tolerable dictionary, so that our language is in a manner barbarous.'

So high is the reputation of Johnson's Dictionary that it has quite overshadowed any of its predecessors, but of course predecessors there were. In 1604 Robert Crawley produced what is possibly the first recognisable English dictionary in his *Table*

Alphabetical but it consisted of only 2543 words, most of which were 'hard words', being, a work, as he announced, intended for 'Ladies, Gentlewomen and any other unskilful person'.

Johnson's most significant precursor was Nathan Bailey's *Universal Etymological English Dictionary* of 1721, an interleaved edition of which was in fact to be Johnson's starting point. A more conveniently sized octavo volume, Bailey's went through 28 editions before the end of the century, and far outsold Johnson's. In the number of entries it also outstrips Johnson, having 60,000 in its 1755 edition, as opposed to Johnson's 45,000, but this is accounted for by the inclusion again of a huge number of 'hard words', for example 'Astramentous: inky'. Although called an Etymological Dictionary, Bailey's is, however, for the most part content with only simplest of definitions: '*Gaggling*: a noise made by geese'; '*Frisky*: leaping and jumping up and down', and with no supporting quotations. For it is in *this*, his inclusion of supportive quotations to bolster his definitions, that Johnson's Dictionary is a landmark in lexicography and literary history, something new and so decisive that in the twentieth century many of his quotations were carried over into the OED.

At the foot of the title page of Johnson's *Dictionary of the English Language* we read 'Printed by W. Strahan for J. and P Knapton; T and T. Longman; C. Hitch and L. Hawes; A. Millar; and R. and J. Dodsley.' These nine men were among the most experienced and influential booksellers and publishers in London. They knew their market and must have been aware for some time of the growing need for an authoritative dictionary. Joseph Addison had given it some serious thought. Even Alexander Pope had toyed with the idea, and drawn up a list of authorities, but was too busy with his translation of Homer to take it any further. What these businessmen, these booksellers and publishers needed was someone who not only had the intellectual ability to undertake the task, but could be counted on to complete it. Their choice of Samuel Johnson looks, in retrospect, to have been the obvious one. But was it?

To the reading public his was not a name that would be instantly recognised. His poem *London* had appeared anonymously as had his *Life of Savage*, and his contributions to *The Gentleman's Magazine* can only be classed as journalism.

When word first reached Johnson that he was to be approached on the subject, he was apparently indifferent. 'I believe I shall not undertake it,' Boswell reports him to have said, but his friend Robert Dodsley, who had published *London*, persuaded him and an agreement was drawn up on 18 June 1746 at The Golden Anchor in Holborn, an agreement which guaranteed Johnson the vast sum of 1500 guineas, a sum which must have been a strong incentive as it meant that he could move into a three-storey spacious house in Gough Square, where the great work began.

Johnson's *Plan for the Dictionary* was published in August 1747 and circulated to attract advance publicity and perhaps to warn off possible competitors. It was written before Johnson had actually begun any work on the Dictionary itself, and seemingly conscious that his qualifications as a lexicographer were open to question

But when he turns to consider what is actually involved in the writing (the word he always uses, not compiling) of a dictionary we realise the extent and depth of his thinking. The first issue a lexicographer must contend with, he recognises, is which words should be included. This was not as simple as it might seem and was a point on which he was prepared to be prescriptive: 'the chief intent of it [the dictionary] is to preserve the purity and ascertain the meaning of our English idiom.' So therefore no 'low terms, the spawn of folly or affectation'? What about 'barbarous and impure words'? And then what about 'Obscure scientific terms'? And at the other end of the scale, when it came to animals, was it worth including *horse, cat* and *dog* when everyone knows what they mean? But what about *crocodile, chameleon*? 'Who shall fix limits on the reader's learning?' he asked, and wisely concluded:

> though the explanations of some [words] may be censured as trivial, because they are almost universally understood, and those of others as unnecessary because they will seldom occur, yet it seems not proper to omit them, since it is rather to be wished that many readers should find more than they expect, than that one should miss what he might hope to find.

It is a dizzying thought that each of the words used to define a given word in a dictionary must themselves be clearly defined in that same dictionary.

Johnson soberly considers the challenges ahead of him. He intends to rationalise spelling, but without introducing unnecessary innovations. Guidance will be given on pronunciation and here again he believes that it is possible to 'fix' it. 'My idea is of an English Dictionary by which the pronunciation of our language may be fixed, and its attainment facilitated, by which its purity may be preserved, its use ascertained and its duration lengthened.' It is a Plan with an agenda. Etymology, one of the weaker aspects of the work, is considered as are certain oddities of grammar: such as that while the plural of *fox* is *foxes* that of *ox* is *oxen*. When it comes to syntax, there is a note of despair 'The syntax of our language is too inconsistent to be reduced to order.' The real challenge, he maintains, and the core of any dictionary, is that of definitions: 'the labour of interpreting these words and phrases, with brevity, fullness and perspicuity' while taking equal note of their possible metaphorical use.

When we come to the citing of authorities, here too there is an agenda. They will not only demonstrate the meaning, but will provide 'such sentences, as besides their immediate use, may give pleasure or instruction by conveying some elegance of language, or some precepts of prudence, or piety.'

While the Plan outlines his aims, intentions and beliefs, the actuality of writing it found him having to change his mind on what had seemed fundamental issues. His initial method of working proved to have been misdirected and needed a whole new approach. From Boswell's account one might believe that the project all went swimmingly:

> The words, partly taken from other dictionaries, and partly supplied by himself, having been first written down with spaces left between them, he delivered in writing their etymologies, definitions and various significations. The authorities were copied from the books themselves, in which he had marked the passages.

What could be simpler? Compile a secondhand wordlist, come up with some definitions and then go looking for appropriate quotations. But a moment's thought shows that such a scheme would never work. If we were to begin, for example, with

Aardvark, the pronunciation and definition would take very little time. The etymology would take longer, but even today with Google at our fingertips, the search for an *appropriate* and *illustrative* quotation could keep us occupied for a not inconsiderable length of time. Johnson's Dictionary does not include *Aardvark*, but the letter *A* alone occupies a column and a half and there are 42,772 other entries, supported by some 100,000 quotations taken from over 500 different authors. If the *modus operandi* outlined by Boswell had been adopted, one man's entire lifetime would not have been sufficient.

Paradoxical though it may seem, *reading came first*. Johnson was extraordinarily widely read. He had been a translator, journalist, reviewer and political commentator, before becoming a poet, playwright, biographer, essayist, novelist and philologist. In the early 1740s he had spent two years compiling the four-volume *An Account of the Harleian Library*, in which he catalogued 50,000 books and 250,000 pamphlets.

Johnson's reading for the dictionary was not random. He knew where to look to find quotations which would not only help to explain the meanings but would, as intended 'give pleasure or instruction, by conveying some elegance of language, or some precept of prudence or piety.' The Bible alone provided him with 4,617 instances, and many come from Milton, Dryden, Pope, and of course Shakespeare.

Bishop Thomas Percy, more conversant with Johnson's work method than Boswell, explains that when Johnson had located a phrase which met his needs he underlined the appropriate word in the book, then wrote its first letter in the margin and with bold vertical lines marked off the beginning and end of the phrase or sentence he wanted to be included. Percy adds that Johnson would ultimately look in other dictionaries 'to see if any words had escaped him, but this, which Mr Boswell makes the first step in the business, was in reality the last'.

The marks Johnson made were in thick black pencil and as there were sometimes three or four such notations to a page, the books were soon rendered useless. His workroom has been described as 'an abattoir of books'. He did suggest that the marks could be removed by rubbing the pages with breadcrumbs, as though that would have helped. Small wonder that people were loath to lend him books, or that Garrick refused point blank to let him anywhere near his Shakespeare Folios.

The books were passed to his amanuenses who copied the marked-up passages into notebooks, leaving gaps for Johnson to add the definitions, etc, but the gaps had to be estimated and were frequently not big enough so that additions had to be squeezed in. And how were the notebooks – there were eventually 80 of them – to be delivered to the printer? After some three years' work, he had the notebooks copied out onto single sheets of paper, but even then the printers refused to work with pages written on both sides.

There was a further delay as the booksellers did not think that plain *Samuel Johnson* on the title page was enough, a view shared by Johnson himself. The Legates of Oxford University were petitioned to award him an honorary A.M. (*Artium Magister*) but as he had left without taking a degree they were at first very reluctant. However, on 20 February 1755 he received their blessing on what has been described as 'a scruffily handwritten Latin document on a ruled sheet not unlike a leaf from a child's exercise book', but it bore the seal and that was enough.

In the November of the previous year, word would seem to have reached Lord Chesterfield that the great work was near completion and he appears to have thought that having it dedicated to him was rather a fine idea. Back in 1747, Johnson's *Plan* had taken the form of a letter to him, and Chesterfield had rewarded him with a gift of £10, but that had been the end of his interest in the project.

Whatever the cause, Johnson's rancour had grown over the years. In a *Rambler* essay of March 1751 we read, 'To solicit patronage is ... to set virtue for sale ... few can be praised without falsehood ... and none can be servile without corruption.' And in the 1755 second edition of *The Vanity of Human Wishes* the torments which await the young scholar: 'Toil, envy, want, the garret and the jail' are amended significantly to: 'Toil, envy, want, the patron and the jail.' And the last nail in the patron's coffin is in the Dictionary's definition: ' ... a wretch who supports with insolence, and is paid with flattery.'

Had Chesterfield not been so full of his own affairs he might have foreseen the trap he was setting up for himself when in November 1754 he published two smugly self-satisfied articles in *The World* in which he as good as declared that as Johnson's patron he was expecting the Dictionary to be dedicated to him.

Dodsley, still of the opinion that Chesterfield's endorsement would be of some advantage, tried to pacify Johnson and in doing so failed to recognise that the letter which His Lordship received on 7 February 1755 was to become one of the most famous of all Johnson's writings and, as its existence soon became widely known, possibly the finest piece of advertising he could ever have hoped for.

Famous though it is, Johnson's letter to Lord Chesterfield simply has to be quoted again, and in all its masterful entirety:

> My Lord,
>
> I have been lately informed by the proprietor of *The World*, that two papers, in which my Dictionary is recommended to the public were written by your Lordship. To be so distinguished, is an honour, which being very little accustomed to favours from the great, I know not well how to receive, or in what terms to acknowledge.
>
> When upon some slight encouragement, I first visited your Lordship, I was overpowered like the rest of mankind, by the enchantment of your address and could not forbear that I might boast myself *Le Vainqueur du vainqueur de la terre* – that I might obtain that regard for which I saw the whole world contending; but I found my attendance so little encouraged, that neither pride nor modesty would suffer me to continue it. When I had once addressed your Lordship in public, I had exhausted all the art of pleasing which a retired and uncourtly scholar can possess. I had done all that I could, and no man is pleased to have his all neglected; be it ever so little. Seven years have now past, my Lord, since I waited in your outward rooms, or was repulsed from your door, during which time I have been pushing on my work through difficulties, of which it is useless to complain, and have brought it, at last, to the verge of publication without one act of assistance, one word of encouragement, or one smile of favour. Such treatment I did not expect, for I never had a Patron before.
>
> Is not a Patron, my Lord, one who looks with unconcern on a man struggling for life in the water, and when he has reached ground, encumbers him with help? The notice which you have been pleased to take of my labours, had it been early, had been kind, but it has been delayed till I am indifferent, and cannot

enjoy it; till I am solitary and cannot impart it; till I am known and do not want it.

I hope it is no very cynical asperity not to express obligation where no benefit has been received, or to be unwilling that the public should consider me as owing that to a Patron, which Providence has enabled me to do for myself. Having carried on my work thus far with so little obligation to any favourer of learning, I shall not be disappointed though I should conclude it, if less be possible, with less; for I have been long wakened from that dream of hope in which I once boasted myself with so much exultation, my Lord, your

Lordship's most humble, most obedient servant,

Sam. Johnson

***

15 April 1755 was publication day and 2000 copies were printed in a two-volume edition, 'bound in boards' and priced at £4. 10s. A large sum, but it was a very large book, weighing close on 20 pounds.

Those who could afford it would have been well-pleased with their purchase. The *Gentleman's Magazine* celebrated it in an eight-page review, but there has always been a problem, as Coleridge saw, observing that 'it was a most instructive and entertaining *book*, but no philosophic and thorough scholar would praise it as a Dictionary.' What he was objecting to was Johnson's high visibility as its author. and that is the problem. Johnson had produced a work the greatness of which is, in the main, due to the fact that he stamped it with his own authority and his own personality. But it was a personality which, it is undeniable, had its quirks and the quirks show. Any mention of his Dictionary is now sure to call to mind, almost immediately, his definition of *Oats: A grain which in England is generally given to horses, but in Scotland supports the people.* There are others just as notorious and they do not have to be looked for, as it was in fact Boswell who very kindly first listed them for us:

> His introducing his own opinions, and even prejudices, under general definitions of words, while at the same time the original meaning of the words is not explained, as his *Tory, Whig, Pension, Oats, Excise,* and a few more, cannot be fully defended, and must be placed to the account of capricious and humorous indulgence.

But it is sad to think that a work of such outstanding intellectual achievement should have come to be known for some half dozen or so of such definitions out of a total of over 40,000.

To take, for example, the verb *To Take.* It is one of the commonest words of the language. What needs to be said about it? Yet, when we turn to Johnson's entry we find that it takes up over five pages, covering 134 different senses of the word and amounts to over 8,000 words. Half a dozen of Johnson's examples will be enough to demonstrate the wide variety of uses we put this commonplace word to.

1. This man always *takes* time and ponders things maturely.
2. *Taking* leave of them I went into Macedonia.
3. I have *taken* her to me for wife.
4. He *took* the dimensions of the room.
5. Thou shalt not *take* the name of the Lord in vain
6. You doubt his sex and take him for a girl.

And the same can be done for other *simple* words such as *put* and *stand.*

1. I charge thee *stand* and tell thy name.
2. He neither *stands* in need of logic, nor uses it.

There are times, it is true, when the whole task seems to have been too tedious to bother with and we find the first definition of *Thick* is *Not thin* only to turn the page and find that *Thin* is *Not thick*. But he does not shy away from those awkward prepositions such as *for, in* and *up*. And it is here that we see the brilliant brevity and succinctness of some of his definitions. *For: the word by which the reason is introduced of something advanced before.* In: *Noting the place where anything is present.* The clarity of the thinking here is quite astonishing, and while the definition of simple things can be complex, so too, of course can be the definition of complex things.

It was an age when great advances were being made in scientific discovery and thinking and Johnson was doing his best to keep up with them as can be seen by his use of quotations from Bacon, Newton, Boyle and Hooke. Among the scientific terms dealt with knowledgeably are *atom, fossil, gravity* and *electricity*. Not included of course is *Oxygen*, as it was not discovered until 1773, but the related 'element' *Phlogiston* is, though it was soon to be established that there was in fact no such thing. There is no reason why Johnson should not have believed in it at the time, but it is good to see that in later editions he thought better of keeping the rather astonishing information that 'In copulation the female [elephant] receives the male lying upon her back and such is his pudicity that he never covers the female so long as anyone appears in sight.' Small wonder then that no one had actually seen them doing so.

Also corrected was his notorious error in the definition of a horse's pastern bone, an error which he explained to his complainant with the famous confession, 'Ignorance, ma'am, pure ignorance.' Equally famous is his response to the ladies who congratulated him on not including any naughty words. 'What, my dears?' he said. 'Then you have been looking for them.'

Some bizarre definitions remain. '*Tarantula*: an insect whose bite can only be cured by music.' The definition being followed by an equally bizarre quotation from John Locke, 'He who uses the word *tarantula*, without having any idea what it stands for, means nothing at all by it.' It is a shame, I think, that later editions did not tell us that 'Cucumbers should be well-sliced, and dressed with pepper and vinegar, and then thrown out, as good for nothing.' It is good, however, to see that he retained the wonderful quotation from Dryden's *Georgics*:

> How cucumbers along the surface creep
> With crooked bodies and with bellies deep.

Such quirks, oddities, eccentricities and jokes stamp the Dictionary as being the work of one man, but putting them aside, the outstanding and unparalleled achievement of that man was his use of quotations. It is hard to believe the reading and research which must have gone into Johnson's compilation of so many authorities and to his great credit the OED editors retained 1700 of them. The King James Bible was his greatest source, providing him with 4,617 entries, but 500 other authors are represented, among them being Shakespeare, Dryden, Locke, Addison and Pope. Even in writing his Dictionary, the didactic element was never far from his mind. He concentrates on what he regarded as the 'best' authors. It was for this reason that he deliberately excluded anything from Hobbes or Shaftesbury, explaining to Mrs Thrale that he would 'never cite any wicked writer's authority for a word, lest it should lead people to look in a book that might injure them for ever.'

With the etymological element completed, it only remained for Johnson to add a History of the Language, a Grammar and a Preface. Neither the Grammar nor the History will have detained many readers over the years, but the *Preface* is among Johnson's finest pieces of writing. He explains and outlines in close detail the principles which determined the orthography, the etymologies and his choice of authorities, but what is most interesting is the way we see how his attitude towards language as a whole had changed over the years. In the initial *Plan* his ambition had been to *ascertain* and fix the language and in the opening of the Preface we are reminded of that:

> When I took the first survey of my undertaking, I found our speech copious without order, and energetic without rules: wherever I turned my view, there was perplexity to be disentangled, and confusion to be regulated; choice was to be made out of boundless variety.

But practice revealed to him that everyday verbs such as *get*, *do*, *put* and *take* 'are hourly shifting their relations, and can no more be ascertained in a dictionary than a grove in the agitation of storm, can be accurately delineated from its picture in the water'. The very word *ascertain* shows the problem. For Johnson it meant *to fix, to make certain*, whereas it now means *to try to find out*. An immense shift in meaning. He later sums up the situation and what his earlier thinking had been:

Those who have been persuaded to think well of my design, will require that it should fix our language and put a stop to those alterations which time and chance have hitherto been suffered to make in it without opposition. With this consequence I will confess that I flattered myself for a while, but now begin to fear that I have indulged expectation which neither reason nor experience can justify.

The *Preface* ends with one of the most personal and moving paragraphs Johnson ever wrote. He admits that his Dictionary will contain errors but concludes

... the world is little solicitous to know whence proceeded the faults of that which it condemns, yet it may gratify curiosity to inform it, that the English Dictionary was written with little assistance of the learned, and without any patronage of the great, not in the soft obscurities of retirement, or under the shelter of academic bowers, but amidst inconvenience and distraction, in sickness and in sorrow ... I have protracted my work till most of those whom I wished to please have sunk into the grave, and success and miscarriage are empty sounds.

Johnson suffered visits from the Black Dog of melancholia throughout his life, but this, one feels, is an example of that melancholia which follows the realisation of a great project, for, as he himself observed in *Rambler* 71 'the completion of almost every wish is found a disappointment.'

4

THE ESSAYIST

IT IS PROBABLE THAT FEW READERS, coming to the end of his Preface to the Dictionary, would have fully appreciated the depth and sincerity of Johnson's feelings when he wrote that he had completed it, 'amidst inconvenience and distraction, in sickness and in sorrow and when most whom I wished to please have sunk into the grave.' But in the minds of those closest to him those words would most likely have stirred memories of his late wife Elizabeth, or Tetty, as he always called her.

Johnson's marriage has always been something of a mystery. On his wedding day in 1735 he was 26 and his bride, a widow with two grown-up children, was 46. Her son, John Porter, vowed never to see her again if she went ahead with the marriage – a vow he kept. And her daughter, Lucy, never forgave him for squandering her mother's money – some £600 – on failed projects to set up a school.

John Taylor, a close associate of Johnson, later told some friends that Tetty was, 'the plague of Johnson's life, was abominably drunken and despicable and that Johnson had frequently complained to him of the wretchedness of his situation with such a wife.' Added to her drink problem, she developed a hypochondria which could only be 'cured' by opium. The rent – she lived separately in Hampstead – the drink and the opium, all added together must have been a heavy drain on his very limited resources.

Tetty died in 1752 and though Johnson did not attend her funeral, he was distraught and ever after in his diaries commemorated her death with entries such as, 'Thought on Tetty, poor dear Tetty with my eyes full.'

It was during these 'inconveniences and distractions' that he was working on the Dictionary and while the initial advance had seemed generous, his false start meant that it was taking far longer than he had estimated. Inevitably funds began running low. He needed money and not being a 'blockhead' he knew that the only solution was more writing.

And so began the essays, written first under the pseudonym of *The Rambler* (1750-52) followed by *The Adventurer* (1753-54) and finally *The Idler* (1758-60) making a total of 323 essays and over 400,000 words.

The first issue of *The Rambler* appeared on Tuesday 28 March 1750. It was a six-page folio pamphlet costing two pence and for which Johnson was paid two guineas. The second issue appeared on the following Saturday and so it continued, twice weekly for two years with Johnson himself writing all but five of the 208 essays. It ceased publication on 14 March 1752, three days before the death of his wife.

Later in life and looking back on his *Rambler* essays, Johnson knew their worth, and was aware of what he had achieved. Samuel Rogers in his *Table Talk* records him as saying, 'My other works are wine and water, but my *Rambler* pure wine'. However, he was also aware that he had never achieved popular success. When it came to essays, the style and tone had been set by Addison and Steele and subsequently eighteenth-century readers knew what to expect and expected what they knew, but with the *Rambler* that is not what they got. There had been a certain intimacy of tone in Addison's *Spectator*; it playfully mocked the fashions and behaviour of those habitués of the coffee-house in which it was claimed the essays were written. *The Spectator* set out to entertain its readers, whereas *The Rambler*, as often as not, made them feel uncomfortable. Addison, as it has often been noted, wrote like a gentleman, Johnson like a teacher. Or, as Lady Mary Wortley Montagu put it more spitefully, '*The Rambler* followed *The Spectator* with the same pace a packhorse would do a hunter.' Indeed it has often been said that *The Rambler* is *The Vanity of Human Wishes* written out in prose.

Johnson was well aware of what his critics were soon saying of him. As early as *Rambler* 23 he admits that they, 'soon began to remark that he [Mr Rambler] was a solemn, serious, dictatorial writer without sprightliness or gaiety and called out with vehemence for more humour.' The list of complaints goes on. But does he propose to change? 'I can without scruple neglect them, and endeavour to gain the favour of the public by following the direction of my own reason, and indulging the sallies of my own imagination.'

The freedom of being able to go his own way twice a week would have been a delight while working on what must at times have been the treadmill of lexicography. He could say what he wanted and he did, which makes one wonder if Tetty had really read *all* the pages, as he had a lot to say about matrimony, and very little of it was positive.

As early as *Rambler* 18 we find him asserting that marriage is, 'very often the cause of misery, and that those who enter into that state can seldom forbear to express their repentance' and he then backs up this assertion with five examples of men whom he claims to have known who made disastrous choices. Among them is one who fell in love with a quiet country girl, who, when he took her to town, 'was expensive in her diversions, vehement in her passions, insatiable of pleasure however dangerous to her reputation and eager of applause by whomsoever it might be given.'

He does concede however that as most writers are men it is inevitable that their view should predominate and in *Rambler* 39 he takes the unusual step of looking at marriage from the woman's point of view.

> The miseries, indeed, which many ladies suffer under conjugal vexations are to be considered with great pity, because their husbands are often not taken by them as objects of affection, but forced upon them by authority and violence ... and it very seldom appears that those who are thus despotic in the disposal of their children pay any regard to their domestic and personal felicity or think it so much to whether they will be happy as to whether they will be rich.

Such sentiments must have rung true with many of his female readers and perhaps, it is to be hoped, caused some fathers to think twice, if it was not too late.

On another occasion he did suggest that marriage could not be, 'entirely miserable, since we see such numbers whom the death of their partner has set free from it, entering it again.' Yet he also argued that a second marriage, an event he had himself had briefly contemplated, was an example of 'the triumph of hope over experience.'

Another of Johnson's sayings which 'everybody knows' is his outburst against women preaching, ' ... like a dog walking on its hinder legs. It is not done well, but you are surprised to find it done at all.' This would suggest a curmudgeonly antifeminist, but it is never a good idea to generalise about Johnson.

Mocking young women for their affectation, their extravagance, vanity and silliness was a standard feature of the eighteenth-century essay. It is to be found time and again in *The Spectator* and was given a monumental boost by Pope's *The Rape of the Lock*. Such mockery is evident in *The Rambler*, but, interestingly, it is never in Johnson's own *Rambler* voice. Instead we find it in the supposed letters he claims to have received from his young women readers themselves. It is not Johnson, one might argue, who is critical of them therefore; the girls condemn themselves, as in the case of *Bellaria* (*Rambler* 191) whose letter begins:

> Dear Mr Rambler,
> I have been four days confined to my chamber with a cold, which has already kept me from three plays, nine sales, five shows, and six card tables and put me seventeen visits behind-hand; and the doctor tells my mamma, that if I fret and cry, it will settle in my head, and I shall not be fit to be seen these six weeks. But dear Mr *Rambler* how can I help it? At this very time *Melissa* is dancing with the prettiest gentleman; – she will breakfast with him tomorrow, and then run to two auctions, and hear compliments,

and have presents, then she will be drest, and visit, and get a ticket to the play; then go to cards, and win, and come home with two flambeaus before her chair. Dear Mr *Rambler*, who can bear it?

It is in his *own* voice, significantly, that we hear him repeatedly arguing for the education of women and deploring a society which seems to see them and value them only as breeding stock or providers of dowries.

We have already seen evidence of Johnson's sympathy for young women who were sold into marriages not of their own choosing, but it is not just sympathy or even pity, but sheer outrage he feels for the fate of girls, often serving maids, debauched and abandoned by their employers and reduced to prostitution. In November 1751 (*Ramblers* 170 & 171) he included two long letters purporting to have come from *Misella*, who tells just such a story, concluding:

> In this abject state I have now passed four years, the drudge of extortion and the sport of drunkenness, sometimes the property of one man, and sometimes the common prey of accidental lewdness; at one time tricked up for sale by the mistress of a brothel, at another begging in the streets to be relieved from hunger by wickedness.

If he seems somewhat out of step with accepted opinion in his attitude towards women, Johnson is even more so when it comes to his views on crime and punishment. In *Rambler* 141 (April 1751) his tone is assertive, one might say aggressive. He begins by pointing out the attraction of power and authority and the perverted pleasure that can be had by those able to assert it; 'political arrogance' as he so rightly calls it.

> It may, I think, be suspected that this political arrogance has sometimes found its way into legislative assemblies ... A slight perusal of the laws by which the measures of vindictive and coercive justice are established, will discover so many disproportions between crimes and punishments, such capricious distinctions of guilt, and such confusion of remissness and and severity, as can scarcely be believed to have been produced by public wisdom, sincerely and calmly studious of public happiness.

One can understand what he means on learning that there were over 200 capital offences on the statute books at that time and that Grand Larceny was defined as the theft of property worth more than twelve pence. He does not mince his words: 'legal massacre' he calls it and asks how many of those eager to watch such executions could claim to have lived lives of total innocence:

> On the days when the prisons of this city are emptied into the grave, let every spectator of the dreadful procession put the same question to his own heart. Few among those that crowd in thousands to the legal massacre, and look with carelessness, perhaps with triumph, on the utmost exacerbations of human misery would then be able to return without horror and rejection.

It would be interesting to know how the far-from-blameless Boswell reacted to this paper, as he hardly ever missed an execution and would often manage to gain an early entrance to the prisons so he could mingle with the men and women about to be brought out to die and always ensured that he had a close and uninterrupted view of their hanging.

Capital punishment was meant to be a deterrent. As the Marquis of Halifax once observed, 'Men are not hanged for stealing horses, but that horses may not be stolen.' But Johnson's view of the matter was bluntly pragmatic:

> The gibbet, indeed, certainly disables those who die upon it from infesting the community; but their death seems not to contribute more to the reformation of their associates than any other method of separation.

Only too aware of the logic in the words, 'as well be hanged for a sheep as a lamb', he suggested that many a thief had gone on to commit murder in the hope of escaping, knowing that if caught he wold hang anyway. 'To equal robbery with murder is to reduce murder to robbery, to confound in common minds the gravity of iniquity and incite the commission of a greater crime to prevent the detection of a less.'

The argument seems to us irrefutable, but he knew perfectly well that it was a hopeless proposition, 'so remote from common practice that I might reasonably fear to expose it to the public.' Hopeless, but one cannot help but admire the compassion and strength of feeling which prompted him to voice it.

But social criticism was not Johnson's chief concern in *The Rambler*. As he said in his final paper, 'I shall never envy the honours which wit and learning obtain in any other cause, if I can be numbered among the writers who have given ardour to virtue, and confidence to truth.'

In *Rambler* 4 he considers the new directions that the novel was taking, thinking particularly, according to Arthur Murphy, of *Roderick Random* and *Tom Jones*. In his opening remarks he seems to be celebrating the new concern with things which 'daily happen in the world', the novelists' 'accurate observation of the living world', but he then argues that therein lies the danger. Such works are aimed at 'the young, the ignorant and the idle to whom they serve as lectures of conduct and instructions into life.' He accepts that art must imitate nature, but 'it is necessary to distinguish those parts of nature which are most proper for imitation'. The young need protection: 'nothing indecent should be suffered to approach their eyes or ears.'

Those who had been readers of *The Rambler* from the outset knew that manners and social criticism, while they certainly concerned him, were far from being his chief concern. That was the fundamental and overriding question: how to achieve a way of life which would bring one true happiness. An odd ambition, it might seem, for someone who had declared in the opening paragraph of his *Life of Savage* that 'the general lot of mankind is misery.' And yet the struggle he put up against his own personal share of that 'general lot' has something quite heroic about it.

A major failing of mankind, Johnson seemed to be saying, is not only our inability to lead a life of virtue, but our inability to live, meaningfully, at all. We are only truly alive for that moment which we call the present, that moment which is *now*. The past is over and done with, beyond change, and the future – even the immediate future – may not contain us. Yet not only do we fail to make full use of *now*, we are, all too often, not even content with it. It is a theme which he developed as early as *Rambler* 2. 'The mind of man is never satisfied with the objects immediately before it, but is always breaking away from the present moment, and losing itself in schemes of future felicity.' The folly and emptiness of such hopes are made plain in *Adventurer* 19. 'Such is the general dream in which we all slumber our time away; every man thinks that time coming in which he shall be gratified with all his wishes ... he dozes away the day in musing upon the morrow, and at the end of life is roused from his dream only to discover that the time of action is past.'

What he is writing about here is what he knows best – aspects of his own life. He had experienced hardship and penury, struggling in those early years in London to gain recognition as a writer and having to endure repeated delays in the staging of his play *Irene*. It was this which allowed him to give personal voice to his recurrent theme: *The Vanity of Human Wishes*. As we have seen, *Rambler* 2 opened with a generalised statement about the dangers of putting one's hopes on the chimera of 'future felicity', but in its closing paragraphs it becomes more specific. 'Perhaps no class of the human species requires more to be cautioned against this anticipation of happiness than those that aspire to the name of authors'. It is worth noting that he uses the word 'aspire'.

It is the folly of such hope and the likelihood of failure that he dwells on at length in *Rambler* 106. 'No place affords a more striking conviction of the vanity of human hopes than a public library; for who can see the wall crowded on every side by mighty volumes, the works of laborious meditation, and accurate enquiry, now scarcely known but by the catalogue.' He goes even further. 'Of the innumerable authors whose performances are thus treasured up in magnificent obscurity, most are forgotten, because they never deserved to be remembered.'

While Johnson shows a keen awareness of the hazards of authors, it is not so clear that he understands those of readers. We are likely to stumble over such words as *frigorifick* and stub our toes against the likes of *adscititious* and *equiponderant*. And we are tempted to agree with the suggestion that he wrote his essays in such a way that his nonplussed and moithered readers would need to buy his dictionary to follow them.

The distinctive prose style of his *Rambler* essays has come in for some harsh criticism, mimicry and ridicule. Macaulay was damning and cruel. 'All his books are written in a learned language; a language which nobody hears from his mother or his nurse; a language in which nobody ever quarrels, or drives bargains, or makes love, a language in which nobody ever thinks.'

Such opinions were being voiced in Johnson's own day, as Boswell admits. 'The style of this work has been censured by some shallow critics as involved and turgid, and abounding with antiquated and hard words.' Johnson defended himself against such charges in his final *Rambler* paper, claiming 'I have laboured to refine our language to grammatical purity and to clear it from colloquial barbarisms, licentious idioms, and irregular combinations.'

It is not that Johnson could not write simply and directly; he could, as we often see in his letters. A letter to Hill Boothby written in December 1755 begins: 'It is midnight and I am again alone. With what meditation shall I amuse this waste hour of darkness and vacuity? If I turn my thoughts upon myself what do I perceive but a poor helpless being reduced by a blast of wind to weakness and misery.' No one who had read only his *Rambler* essays could believe this was written by the same man, but when it came to addressing the public at large or – to use his own phrase – the general reader, he would climb back up on his stilts again and stride loftily and awkwardly about.

This last of Johnson's *Rambler* essays was dated 14 March 1752. Later that year his friend Dr John Hawkesworth, a fellow member of the Ivy Lane Club, launched a new magazine, *The Adventurer*. Its first issue came out on 7 November. A great admirer of *The Rambler*, Hawkesworth persuaded Johnson, who was again short of money, to become a collaborator.

The title, we need to keep in mind, was Hawkesworth's, not Johnson's, or we might think that Mr Rambler had given up his casual strolls and was boldly striking out in a new direction and now working on a wider range of topics, but this was not to be. Having written some two hundred *Ramblers*, it came all too easily to him, and in several of the *Adventurer* pieces he seems to be doing no more than going through the motions. There is a mechanical feel to it and several of the topics are ones he has dealt with before. The opening sentence is all too familiar: 'To a benevolent disposition, every state of life will afford some opportunities of contributing to the welfare of mankind.' It purports to be a letter from the Fleet Prison in which someone calling himself Misargyrus recounts his Rake's Progress of a life so as to point to the failings of the social and prison system. It is all too predictable, as is his lengthy sequel, printed three weeks later and yet another in June.

In another instance, *Adventurer* 84, in order to demonstrate the folly of false pretensions, we are told of a group of people travelling together in a coach, each of whom claims to be more significant than they actually are. Again it is predictable. Their folly is eventually revealed, but the dénouement (if one might call it such) is no surprise at all. Narrative was never a strong point with Johnson.

It is a dull collection, repeating much of what had already appeared in *The Rambler*. How many times do we need to be reminded of the vanity of human wishes, of the 'general dream in which we all slumber out our time: every man thinks the day coming in which he shall be gratified with all his wishes'?

Not even in his essay published on 25 December 1753 does he wish his readers a Merry Christmas or even the compliments of the season. Instead they are warned that, 'Inordinate desires, of whatever kind, ought to be repressed upon yet a higher consideration; they must be considered as enemies not only to happiness but to virtue.'

Saturday 2 March 1754 saw the last of these *Adventurer* essays and on 15 April of the following year the great Dictionary was published, but it was another three years after that before Johnson took up his pen again as an essay writer, this time under the name of *The Idler*. Just as it is thought that his *Rambler* essays provided him with a welcome break from the mechanical drudgery of the Dictionary and *The Adventurer* provided him with an equally welcome addition to his finances, so it is possible that the freedom which he allowed himself in *The Idler* made a change from the close work that his edition of Shakespeare entailed, the Proposals for which had appeared two years before. He may also have been unable to resist the persuasive powers of John Newbery, an enthusiastic publisher of genius.

The *Universal Chronicle*, published every Saturday, featured Johnson's *Idler* essay on its front page, and might have been intended primarily as a vehicle for Johnson, as when he ended his contributions on 5 April 1760, so too ended the *Universal Chronicle*.

The chief concern of Johnson's opening essay is his new pen-name. 'Every man is, or hopes to be, an Idler,' he says, explaining that 'as peace is the end of war, so to be idle is the ultimate purpose of the busy', and, he continues, 'it is a sensible aim as the Idler has no rival or enemies.' In addition, he claims, 'man is the only being that can properly be called idle, that does by others what he might do himself.'

We instantly recognise that these are arguments which lack the high moral seriousness of *The Rambler* and they would have seemed very strange to those who recalled the *Rambler* essay of June 1751 in which he had argued strongly against idleness as a sin, and a sin of which he had often accused himself, as Boswell tells us. There is no way that one can argue against his contention that 'the certainty that life cannot be long and the probability that it will be much shorter than nature allows, ought to awaken every man to the active prosecution of whatever he is desirous to perform.' It is abundantly clear that the contrast between the two attitudes and beliefs is matched only by the contrast in their expression. Johnson the Idler is a different man, an older man. It is not that he lacks the aggressive self-assurance of his earlier days, rather that he is now so self-assured that he does not feel the need to show it. He is now *Dr Johnson*, a man who has accomplished something, is known and recognised for his accomplishment and is respected. He can afford to take himself a little less seriously and this might possibly have been suggested to him by Newbery who knew the market better than anybody. The market was important, as by their agreement Johnson was to share the profits rather than have a flat fee per issue.

Apart from an impassioned attack in No 17 against vivisection and those 'whose favourite amusement is to nail dogs to tables and open them alive', most of the earlier essays are somewhat bland and lightweight. He argues that there are already too many writers. In another essay he purports to see no reason why women should not be soldiers, though he had previously insisted that they could not be preachers. There is a spoof from a 'real idler' and a piece on the effect of the weather on our moods. There are some splendid moments, of course, such as the suggestion that 'the compilation of newspapers is often committed to narrow and mercenary minds.' Surely not!

Things went on in this bland way for almost five months which is possibly why *The Idler* essays have attracted so few readers and so little critical attention. But then in September 1758 something – possibly the humiliating defeat of the British army by the French in the Battle of Ticonderoga – seems to have shaken Johnson up and his essay No 22 was such a biting anti-war satire that it was thought to be too seditious to be included in the collected edition and in its place he inserted a piece on the evils of debtors' prisons, a topic he had already covered more than once in the past and on which he had little or nothing new to say.

And when in essay 24, 'On Thinking', we find ourselves reading, 'He that lives in torpid insensibility wants nothing of a carcass but putrefaction', we recognise that we are momentarily back in the company of someone we know.

Just as Johnson gave us a self-portrait in *The Rambler*, so the foibles of 'my old friend Sober' in *Idler* 31 are clearly those of Johnson himself. The topic is once again idleness and the suggestion is made that one way of passing time is 'to fill each day with petty business; to have always something to hand.'

Sober's chief pleasure, like that of his creator, is 'conversation; there is no end of his talk or his attention' but when he must go home that his friends may sleep, then come those 'moments of which poor Sober trembles at the thought', a feeling Johnson knew only too well.

Many 'petty businesses' are listed by which they both pass the time, but the most intriguing of all is his 'daily amusement of chymistry'. We recall Boswell telling us several times that 'Chymistry was always an interesting pursuit with Dr Johnson. And Mr Sober has a small furnace, which he employs in distillation, and which has long been the solace of his life.'

The tone of *The Idler* is far lighter than that of the earlier essays. We feel that Johnson is speaking to us from his fireside rather than haranguing us from his soapbox. There is far less moralising, but now and then we are treated to maxims of proverbial wisdom: 'nothing is more hopeless than a scheme of merriment ... the rich and the powerful dwell in a perpetual masquerade.' That has never been put more brilliantly or more succinctly.

The Idler gives us more frequent glimpses into the social life of the age. In No 78 he recounts a visit to a spa, 'one of those places to which a mineral spring gives the idle and luxurious an annual reason for resorting' and tells us of the various habitués he had encountered, especially memorable being Tom Steady, an opinionated bore whose endless babble Johnson parodies brilliantly.

The *Idler* essays are so fascinatingly varied one cannot guess what is coming next. One could never have guessed until reading No 40 that duvets were on sale in the middle of the eighteenth century and being marketed with the advertising slogan 'Warmer than four or five blankets, yet lighter than one!'

The unpredictability factor must have been one of the attractions for those first readers of the *Universal Chronicle* and nowhere is this better demonstrated than where the questionable morality of advertising is followed by a moving piece on the death of his mother, an essay which evokes the most tender of feelings, while couched in the simplest of language. The grief is evident and equally so is Johnson's deep dread of death.

> Yet such is the course of nature that whoever lives long must outlive those whom he loves and honours. Such is the condition of our present existence, that life must one time lose its associations and every inhabitant of the earth must walk downward to the grave alone and unregarded, without any partner of his joy or grief, without any interested witness of his misfortunes or success.

It is this fear of death, the final ending, which makes Johnson's last *Idler* essay so incomparably moving. It was published on Saturday 5 April 1760 and as Johnson pointed out 'in that solemn week which the Christian world has always set apart for the examination of the conscience, the review of life, the extinction of earthly desires and the renovation of holy purposes.' It is an essay which needs to be read in its entirety, but one paragraph will have to suffice.

> The secret horror of the last is inseparable from a thinking being whose life is limited and to whom death is dreadful. We always make a secret comparison between the part and the whole; the termination of any period of life reminds us that life itself has likewise its termination; when we have done anything for the last time we involuntarily reflect that a part of the days allotted us is past, and that as more is past there is less remaining.

5

RASSELAS

THE YEARS AFTER JOHNSON LEFT OXFORD in 1729 were years of failure and melancholy. He went back home to Lichfield where for two years he was probably more of a hindrance than a help in the family bookshop, which eventually failed in 1731 when his father died heavily in debt. The following year he secured the post of usher in a school in Market Bosworth, but failed at that. His school friend Edmund Hector came to his rescue, inviting him to live with him in Birmingham where he had rooms in the house of Thomas Warren, a bookseller who was thinking of going into publishing and it was then, seemingly, that Johnson mentioned a book which he had read while at Pembroke, *A Voyage to Abyssinia* by a Portuguese Jesuit priest Jerome Lobo, who had been sent as a missionary in 1624 to Abyssinia. He was there for nine years and on his return to Portugal wrote an account of his adventures, which Johnson read and which Hector persuaded him to translate.

Johnson's version is a remarkable book, an exciting book. It is a story of adventure and derring-do with hardly a trace of religion in it. Father Lobo suffers all kinds of hardship, enduring extremes of hunger and thirst while crossing desert tracts. He is caught up in the innumerable bloody battles of inter-tribal and religious strife; sees friends beheaded, is threatened with death by impalement or being flayed alive. Inadvertently he eats poisoned berries, is stung by scorpions, bitten by snakes and chased by elephants. Even on his journey home to Portugal, his ship is wrecked and he is captured by Turkish pirates.

Tales of Arabia and the Orient were never a major element in eighteenth-century literature, but they were very popular with the reading public and it must have been this popularity which persuaded Johnson to compose his own Oriental Tale *Rasselas*, which he wrote solely to pay for the funeral expenses of his mother who had died on 21 January 1759 at the age of ninety. It brought him in £100 and he finished it, as he told Reynolds, 'in the evenings of one week'.

Writing in such haste Johnson prudently re-cycled material he had used before. His protagonist's name he had encountered in Lobo's book and he had read there that princes of the blood-royal were kept in close seclusion until chosen to become emperor. Lobo had also described coming across 'a happy place', as he called it, 'an opening between the mountains which heaven seems to have made ... shady trees, a clear stream, and the luxury of a cooling breeze.' These three factors Johnson combined to create his idyllic *Happy Valley* in which Prince Rasselas and his siblings are sequestered.

Viewed from one angle, Johnson would seem to be depicting an earthly paradise. 'From the mountains on every side, rivulets descended that filled all the valley with verdure and fertility ...

the banks of the brooks were diversified with flowers, every blast shook spices from the rocks and every month dropped fruits upon the ground.' And when he tells of the animals we might be looking at William Hicks' *The Peaceable Kingdom*. 'On one part were flocks and herds feeding on the pastures, on another all the beasts of chase frisking in the lawns; the sprightly kid was bounding on the rocks, the subtle monkey frolicking in the trees, and the solemn elephant reposing in the shade.'

But we had been given a clear warning in the opening paragraph:

> Ye who listen with credulity to the whispers of fancy, and pursue with eagerness the phantoms of hope, who expect that age will perform the promises of youth, and that the deficiencies of the present day will be supplied by the morrow; attend to the story of Rasselas, Prince of Abissinia.

He was only too conscious of the 'deficiencies of the present day': it was not simply the death of his mother which grieved him, he had also lost the tenancy of Gough Square, which deprived him of the company of Mrs William and Robert Levet. And his black servant Frank Barber had left to join the navy. For Johnson, who had a fear of solitude and always needed people around him, these must have been depressing days.

And there is throughout much of the early pages of *Rasselas* a scattering of disturbing shadows. As early as the third paragraph we are told that the Prince is *confined* to the Happy Valley, a word with a distinctly threatening tone. And immediately afterwards we learn that the only way in or out of the Valley is 'closed with gates of iron'. Although the Valley is 'filled with delight', the Emperor nevertheless pays a visit once a year to discover if anything could be added to this delight, but the language in which this is couched is full of barbs. Each inhabitant was required 'to propose whatever might contribute to make *seclusion* pleasant, to fill up the *vacancies* of attention and lessen *the tediousness of time.*' Entertainers, musicians and dancers from the outside competed in the hope that they too might be allowed to remain in this *blissful captivity.*

Chapter III introduces us to a different aspect of life in the Valley. Entertainment is not enough to pacify its inhabitants. 'Every art was practised to make them pleased with their own condition.' *Art* and *practised* are loaded words telling of lies and deceit. It is a situation which Johnson develops in his imagination, but one with which we have become all too familiar. They are being brainwashed. There are unnamed *Sages* who 'instructed the inmates, told them of nothing but the miseries of public life, and described all beyond the mountains as regions of calamity, where discord was always raging and where man preyed upon man.' We are reminded of the isolationism of North Korea and in what follows of the use made of art and literature by the old Soviet Union and Chairman Mao's China. 'To heighten their opinion of their own felicity, they were daily entertained with songs, the subject of which was the *happy valley.*' To Johnson this was fiction, it came from his imagination, but when we remember the Happy Valley's wall it is hard not to think of East Germany and when Rasselas calls attention to himself by seeming dissatisfied with all these *delights* then, 'One of the Sages, in whose conversation he had formerly delighted, followed him secretly, in hope of discovering the cause of his disquiet.' *Secretly*, we notice. Johnson's Happy Valley is suddenly all too familiar. These are the tactics of a totalitarian police state; these Sages are the Stasi.

Searching for the cause of his restlessness, Rasselas considers the beasts of the field around him, accepts that they share the same basic needs – feel hunger, thirst, need rest – yet is aware that there is something different; he begins to be aware of a spiritual nature. As he puts it, musing aloud to himself, "'Man has surely some latent sense for which this place affords no gratification, or he has some desires distinct from sense which must be satisfied before he can be happy.'"

Having overheard this, his Stasi-Sage determines to win him back to conformity and puts it to him the next day that, "'If you want for nothing how are you unhappy?'" But that is exactly at the root of the Prince's problem. "'That I know not what I want is the cause of my complaint ... give me something to desire.'" Puzzled by this, the Sage overplays his hand. "'Sir,'" said he, "if you had seen the miseries of the world, you would know how to value your present state.'" And that, as Rasselas immediately sees, is precisely what he wants. "'Now,' said the Prince, "you have given me something to desire; I shall long to see the miseries of the world, since the sight of them is necessary to happiness.'"

He needs to escape from the Happy Valley. But how? The surrounding mountains were too high to scale and the iron door impregnable, so initially his only means of escape was through his imagination. Twenty months, we are told, passed by like this 'since he first *resolved* to escape from his confinement'. What a waste of time, he thought, and once these 'sorrowful meditations fastened upon his mind, he passed four months in *resolving* to lose no more time in idle *resolves*.' The repetition of this word *resolve* cannot be accidental; indeed it rings out at least a score of times throughout this short work.

In his Dictionary Johnson's definitions of the word leave us in no doubt what he meant by it. As a noun it is a *fixed determination*. As a verb *to fix in constancy* and *to decree with oneself.* The irony is clear. Who could be more irresolute and vacillating than Rasselas? His discouragement and dejection are, however, understandable, but at last, we are told, he '*resolved* never to despair' having 'now known the blessing of hope'. And as Johnson had said in *Idler* 58, 'It is necessary to hope, though hope should always be deluded; for hope itself is happiness and its frustrations, however frequent, are less dreadful than its extinction.'

A possible way of escape seems be offered to Rasselas when he finds that one of the artificers in the Valley is at work on a pair of wings which, if successful, would enable him to fly up over the mountains. Unfortunately at the end of the chapter the poor man leaps off a small promontory and promptly falls down into the lake.

As we hear no more about him after this it seems that it was simply an amusing digression, but it may also be seen as the first example, among many, of the folly of unreasonable hope. *Rasselas* contains very little narrative continuity. Each incident is distinct and separate. It is lived through and the protagonists then move on to another without appearing to have been in any way changed by the experience. In this respect it has a picaresque quality. In his *Rambler* essay number 4 Johnson had written tellingly about the advances in contemporary fiction, but does not seem to have been aware that what he was writing was in any way related to what Richardson and Fielding were doing and does not feel it incumbent on him in any way to follow their example. For instance, in the next chapter we meet Imlac who is to play such an important role in all that follows, but we are not told what he looks like, whether he is tall or short, thin or stout – nothing. And this applies to all the characters in the story, including Rasselas himself.

And when they talk they all sound the same – men and women – they all sound like Samuel Johnson.

Imlac is introduced to us as a poet, yet in all his subsequent wanderings we never hear of him writing a poem. It was one he had written earlier which had caught Rasselas's attention – a poem 'upon the various conditions of humanity' which makes it sound rather like Johnson's own *Vanity of Human Wishes*. But what holds his attention is Imlac's knowledge of the outside world and he commands him to tell the story of his life. It is a story which takes up five chapters and seems to have no other purpose than to highlight Rasselas' naivety. As it unfolds he is astonished to learn that governments appear to allow crimes to be committed, and he cannot understand why a wealthy man should want more money or that 'there is such depravity in man that he should injure another.' He frequently doubts what he is hearing, 'I doubt not the facts which you relate, but imagine you impute them to mistaken motives.'

Chapter X comes to us as a total surprise. Its title is 'A Dissertation Upon Poetry' and contains one of the book's most quoted passages:

> The business of a poet, said Imlac, is to examine, not the individual, but the species; to remark general properties and large appearances; he does not number the streaks of the tulip or describe the different shades in the verdure of the forest.

That these are Johnson's own views has sometimes been doubted, but in an *Adventurer* of 1754 we find him arguing against the 'rejection of the common opinion, a defiance of common censure, and an appeal from general laws to private judgement.' The poet must 'consider right and wrong in the abstracted and invariable state ... and rise to general and transcendental truths which will always be the same.' Half a century later Blake would refute this bluntly in his *Annotations to Reynolds*. 'To generalize is to be an idiot,' he wrote. 'To particularize is the Alone Distinction of Merit.' And again, 'Without Minute Neatness of Execution the Sublime cannot Exist!' It is an assertion which is at the core of that change in thinking and expression which became the Romantic movement.

But this debate on what constitutes poetry is brought to an abrupt end by Rasselas, '"Enough! Thou hast convinced me that no human being can ever be a poet. Proceed with thy narration."' Imlac then tells him of his travels through Syria and Palestine, whose people surpass the Europeans for their medicine, their technical achievements and their transport system, prompting Rasselas to declare, '"They are surely happy who have all these conveniences."' But Imlac's unforgettable reply is one of the pivotal moments in the whole work. '"The Europeans are less unhappy than we, but they are not happy. Human life is everywhere a state in which much is to be endured, and little to be enjoyed."'

To which the Prince replies, '"I will open to thee my heart. I have long meditated an escape from the happy valley."' And then he declares a positive *resolve*. '"Whatever be the consequences of my experiment, I am resolved to judge with my own eyes of the various conditions of men, and then to make deliberately my *choice of life*.'" The italics are Johnson's own and point to the original title he had in mind: *The Choice of Life; or the History of Rasselas, Prince of Abyssinia.*

Johnson, we should perhaps concede, is not interested in constructing a narrative, creating a sense of place, developing a character or explaining how events occurred. Such things are passed over as quickly as possible. Once the Prince and Imlac have *resolved* to escape from the Happy Valley, they simply consider how the conies have 'burrowed upwards in an oblique line' and so, procuring (we are not told what or how) 'implements proper to hew stone and remove earth, they fall to their work on the next day.' Nothing, seemingly, could be easier. Accompanying them now are Rasselas's sister Nekayah and her maid Pekuah and our intrepid foursome lose no time at all in sailing to Suez and from 'Suez they travelled by land to Cairo', where 'They studied the language two years, while Imlac was preparing to set before them the various ranks and conditions of mankind.' And that of course is the whole point of their escape and which Johnson wanted to get to as soon as possible. Who cares what sort of ship they sailed on, what the captain's name was, or what the weather was like? There are far more important things to consider: namely *the choice of life*. All that follows is centred on this and is less a narrative than a series of *exempla*.

Convinced that happiness is to be found somewhere, Rasselas *resolves* to abandon the frivolities of pleasure and instead to pursue wisdom. To his great delight he soon encounters a philosopher who powerfully and grandiloquently argues the case for following reason rather than emotion, an attitude which will ensure that man, '"is no longer a slave of fear, nor the fool of hope; is no more emaciated by envy, inflamed by anger, emasculated by tenderness, or depressed by grief.'" Rasselas listened to him 'with veneration', but again Imlac warns him to beware as such men might discourse '"like angels, but they live like men."' It was a warning which proved to be true, as only a few days later Rasselas found his new mentor wildly distraught at the sudden death of his daughter, and quite beyond any possible consolation.

Having thus dramatically dismissed the claims of stoicism, another myth comes under scrutiny: that of the joys of the simple life. The shepherds they meet are, however, so uncouth and ignorant that they learn nothing from them except; that 'their hearts were cankered with discontent; that they considered themselves as condemned to labour for the luxury of the rich, and looked up with stupid malevolence toward those that were placed above them.'

Recognising, it would seem, that the picaresque element was becoming too obvious, Johnson allows the Princess to direct their course. They had lived a very restricted life, she says, and suggests that Rasselas should '"try what is to be found in the splendour of courts, and I will range the shades of humbler life."'

One might have thought that their recent experiences would have shown them the folly of pursuing unreal hopes of happiness, but just as Gulliver sailed off into another disaster, seemingly having learned nothing from his previous voyages, so they are happy to go on hoping and planning – which is, as Johnson is showing us, an essential factor in the human condition.

And so the Prince entered the splendid court of the Bassa, 'whom all approached with reverence and heard with obedience', but found that it was a hotbed of plots, faction and treachery.

Very soon the Bassa was carried off in chains to Constantinople, his successor was deposed and in turn his successor was murdered.

Princess Nekayah fared little better. The young women she met struck her for the most part as vain and empty-headed tittle-tattlers, and there was as much discord, she realised, in little families as in great kingdoms, this being especially true of the antipathy between the young and the old. 'Age looks with anger on the temerity of youth and youth with contempt on the scrupulosity of age.' Domestic discord was so rife, she discovered, that many avoided marriage altogether, but they lived, she observed 'without friendship, without fondness', persuading her to conclude with that famously bleak observation, 'Marriage has many pains, but celibacy has no pleasures.'

Not as yet married themselves, it is understandable that this should be a topic of some interest to these young people, but it is surprising that Johnson has them debate it at far greater length than any other topic. Rasselas thinks his sister 'supposed misery where she did not find it', but in reply she provides a formidable list of the many 'forms of connubial infelicity'. Much of their argument is re-cycled from Johnson's *Rambler* essays and Nekayah is certainly given the stronger case against it.

> What can be expected but disappointment and repentance from a choice made in the immaturity of youth, in the ardour of desire, without judgement, without foresight, without inquiry after conformity of opinions, similarity of manners, rectitude of judgement, or purity of sentiment?

Rasselas is not even given the chance of a further say and the following chapter is headed: 'Imlac enters and changes the conversation'. He puts an end to their discussion by telling them that '"while you are making the choice of life, you neglect to live."' But what he suggests, to Rasselas's surprise, is that they visit Egypt's ancient monuments. And so off they go on a trip to see the Great Pyramid.

Although a keen reader of travel books, Johnson makes no attempt to portray the scene. The geometry and consequent stability of its shape is all we are given, and its interior is equally glossed over as a series of galleries and vaults. Instead, Imlac seizes the opportunity to deliver a lecture on man's perpetual dissatisfaction. It was a structure of no possible use, he argued, and was no more than 'a monument of the insufficiency of human enjoyments.' A ruler of unlimited power had amused 'the tediousness of declining life by seeing thousands labouring without end, and one stone, for no purpose, laid upon another.'

But this series of exempla and lectures is suddenly interrupted by a strain of narrative for, when they climbed out again into the open air they found that the Princess's maid Pekuah was missing. Fearful of the dark and of ghosts, she had begged permission to stay outside, but she and her two maids had been abducted, carried off by Arabs. Nekayah is distraught. Her women try to comfort her, but not, as Johnson wryly observes, 'much grieved in their hearts that the favourite was lost.'

Time went by with Nekayah sinking into 'silent pensiveness and gloomy tranquillity'. But after seven months, news reached them that Pekuah was being held on the borders of Nubia by an Arab chief who was prepared to accept a ransom of 200 ounces of gold. The money was paid, Pekuah restored to them, and all were eager to hear the story of her ordeal.

It is a story with which she then regales them at quite

unexpected and unnecessary length. At first, she says rather coyly, she was fearful of the 'gratification of any ardour or desire' on the part of their captors, but she was treated with great respect. It was, the Arab explained, only the ransom money he was interested in. After weeks of wandering through the desert they came to a spacious house on an island in the River Nile, where the girls in the seraglio were as silly and empty-headed as those the Princess had encountered in Cairo. Nothing in her account is in any way new and coming to an abrupt end it is then forgotten about. It is little more than an interlude and a rather clumsy one indicative of the speed with which Johnson was writing and his failure to give thought to the work's overall design or purpose.

Apropos of nothing, Rasselas suddenly announces that he intends 'to devote himself to science and pass the rest of his days in literary solitude', but Imlac warns him of the dangers of such a resolution by relating the story of an astronomer who spent years in solitary study. He was unquestionably a man of great learning, integrity and generosity, but quite mad, claiming that he alone controlled and regulated the climate of the entire planet, a gift which he wishes to bequeath to Imlac. Rasselas, Nekayah and Pekuah find the idea hilarious, but Imlac is more concerned for him and delivers them a lecture on 'such maladies of the mind.'

Imlac's contention is that, 'All power of fancy over reason is a degree of insanity' and that 'There is no man whose imagination does not sometimes predominate over his reason', going on to assert that, 'By degrees the reign of fancy is confirmed; she grows first imperious and in time despotic.' What he says strikes a chord in each of his listeners. Pekuah confesses that she sometimes imagines herself the Queen of Abyssinia. In contrast the Princess dreams she is a humble shepherdess, while Rasselas's fantasy is that he is the leader of a perfect government. And this, Imlac insists, is one of the dangers of solitude.

But at this point, instead of following up the connection with the astronomer's solitude and his delusions, there comes a totally inexplicable interlude. While they were walking home, we are told, they met up with an old man and enquired what life was like for him. We have already been told in *The Vanity of Human Wishes* that 'Life protracted is protracted woe', so a further tale of woe is what we have come to expect. Declining into decrepitude, as he puts it, all his friends have died and 'nothing new is of much importance', and so he goes off 'leaving his audience not much elated with the hope of long life.'

Returning eventually to the story of the astronomer and agreeing that solitude is the cause of his delusions, they decide to begin paying him visits and eventually encouraging him to leave his house and visit them, and slowly he begins 'to delight in sublunary pleasures.' Their friendship having grown, they ask him for his views on the choice of life and once again it is a tale of disappointment. But the friendship and good company he is now enjoying have their effect. 'Since he had mingled in the gay comforts of life, and divided his hours by a succession of amusements he found the conviction of his authority over the skies fade gradually from his mind.' He is even prepared to suggest what their next amusement should be, suggesting a visit to the catacombs on the grounds that 'answers they can no longer procure from the living, they may be given by the dead'.

Catacombs inevitably lead to a consideration of death and death to thoughts of the afterlife and the nature and existence of the soul. Their sustained debate on the unconsciousness of matter and the immateriality of the mind is sophisticated and complex. It leads us to expect that the work is moving towards a religious conclusion and the final words spoken by the Princess would seem to confirm that. '"To me," said the Princess, "the choice of life has become less important: I hope hereafter to think only on the choice of eternity."' But the final chapter is headed 'The conclusion, in which nothing is concluded.'

In this final chapter the Nile has risen; they are cut off and cannot leave the house. Why they had not foreseen this we are not told, nor why they cannot use a boat. However, confined as they are they pass the time in reminiscence and anticipation, which, as Johnson had earlier said, was the normal state of affairs. They recall the adventures and encounters they have had and discuss the 'various schemes of happiness which each of them had formed.' Pekuah wants to be the prioress of a convent. The Princess wants to found a college of learned woman and Rasselas to govern a little kingdom. Each, it is worth noting, wants power and authority, but Johnson pours cold water on their ambitions. 'Of these wishes that they had formed they well knew that none could be obtained.' As it is clear that they are all equally qualified and capable of filling such a position, it must be the expectation of happiness where the doubt lies. They will not be exempt from the human condition which the preceding chapters have played out for us. They will never be free from upsets and disappointments. They know this themselves and there is in the final sentence a note of defeatism. 'They deliberated a while what was to be done, and resolved (that word again) when the inundation should cease, to return to Abissinia.' They are not, of course, thinking or returning to the Happy Valley; that would be denied them even it was their plan.

The ending has been called pessimistic and a tragic view of life, but those who look for a tidy ending and regret that there is no resolution to the question do not seem to recognise that it is a truthful ending. It is the way things are.

Samuel Beckett, who is recorded as having said, 'It's Johnson, always Johnson who is with me', clearly understood that, and would have us understand it too. In *Waiting for Godot* Vladimir declares, 'Why are we here that is the question. And we are blessed in this that we happen to know the answer. Yes, in this immense confusion one thing alone is clear. We are waiting for Godot to come.' And when Estragon complains, 'I can't go on like this', he is told. 'That's what you think.'

6

THE SCOTTISH TOUR

BOSWELL MUST HAVE THOUGHT THE DAY would never come – he had been suggesting it for so many years – but on 14 August 1773 Johnson at last joined him at his house in St James's Court in Edinburgh. He had set off from London on the 6th and travelled the 390 mile road journey in a post-chaise. It had not been a pleasant journey. Such conveyances never were, even over short distances and Johnson was soon feeling unwell. At York he was, 'much disturbed by old complaints'. But he rested up for three days in Edinburgh and while Boswell ensured that several local worthies came to entertain him, he himself was apparently upsetting and annoying Mrs Boswell. She had long held Johnson largely responsible for the dissolute scrapes her husband got into, even his frequent doses of gonorrhoea, while he was in London. But on the 18 August she was able to wave them off on their tour to the Hebrides and would not see them again until 9 November.

Johnson had harboured a longing to visit the Hebrides since he was a small boy when his bookseller father had put into his hands a copy of Martin Martin's *A Description of the Western Isles of Scotland*. He even packed a copy of the book to take with him. It had been published in 1695, but Johnson seems to have held the somewhat romantic notion that little had changed since then, and even Boswell's account opens with the hope, 'that we might there contemplate a system of life almost totally different from what we had been accustomed to see; and, to find simplicity and wildness, and all the circumstances of remote time and place, so near ... ' The innocence is almost charming.

It was a tour which was to take them up the east coast, past Arbroath and Aberdeen, round the shoulder of the headland up to Banff and on to the top of Loch Ness, which they then followed down to Fort Augustus. From there they headed west, eventually crossing to the Isle of Skye, where bad weather held them for longer than they had planned. From Skye they sailed to Oban, calling at Col, Mull and Iona, then south to Glasgow and on to Auchinleck, the ancestral home of the Boswells and an uneasy encounter with James's father. Finally back to Edinburgh after 83 days and a journey of close on 700 miles. In the later stages it had often been over rough track, heath and bog, which had to be traversed on horseback or on foot. We need to remember that Johnson was 63 when they set out and, as Boswell put it, 'His person was large ... and grown unwieldly from corpulence.' And on top of this, as Boswell solemnly recorded, 'In all September we had one day and a half of fair weather, and October perhaps not more.'

We have three separate accounts of their Tour: Johnson's own *A Journey to the Western Isles of Scotland*, published in 1775, soon after his return, and Boswell's *The Journal of a Tour to the Hebrides with Samuel Johnson, LL.D* which did not appear until 1785, the year after Johnson's death. In addition there are the twenty or so letters which Johnson wrote to Mrs Thrale while he was actually travelling. These letters show that Johnson was not always finding it 'pleasant'. His letter of 30 September, at about the halfway stage begins, 'I am still confined to Skie', and concludes, 'I long to be again at home ... this climate perhaps is not within my degree of healthy latitude.'

That the three versions should differ is not surprising, but the ways in which they do are interesting and at times surprising. One of the most quoted extracts of Johnson's account comes as they are approaching Glensheals. He needed a rest.

> I sat down on a bank, such as a writer of Romance might have delighted to feign. I had indeed no trees to whisper over my head, but a clear rivulet streamed at my feet. The day was calm, the air soft, and all was rudeness, silence, and solitude. Before me, and on either side, were high hills which by hindering the eye from ranging, forced the mind to find entertainment for itself. Whether I spent the hour well I know not; for here I first conceived the thought of this narration.

This passage was singled out by reviewers – possibly because it was so unlike the Johnson they were used to. One hailed it as, 'a fortunate event in the annals of literature.' But we know from Boswell that Johnson had been writing notes long before that time. And when we turn to his letter to Mrs Thrale, he describes the same scene, but adds, 'I looked round me, and wondered that I was not more affected, but the mind is not at all times equally ready to be put in motion.' A certain degree of 'feigning' does seem to have been occasioned in the version meant for the public.

How Johnson reacted to landscape it is hard to gauge, but it is fairly certain he would have found Wordsworth incomprehensible. He could not even share Boswell's enthusiasms. Passing through Glensheal, Boswell remarked on the *immensity* of one of the mountains. It may even have been the spectacular Buchaille Etive Mor, but Johnson dismissed it. 'No, it is no more than a considerable protuberance.' It is possible of course that he was simply being provocative, but there are other occasions when he clearly lacks the vocabulary to recreate a scene for his readers. Another of the area's outstandingly beautiful features is the *Buller of Buchan* and, although Johnson allowed that it was something 'which no man can see with indifference', he went on to describe it as 'a rock perpendicularly tabulated.'

The eighteenth-century philologist James Burnett, Lord Monboddo, admittedly no friend of Johnson, objected to 'the richness' of the language in his *Journey*. Johnson was quick to defend himself, 'Why, Sir, this criticism would be just if in my style, superfluous words, or words too big for the thought could be pointed at, but this, I believe, cannot be done.' In fact it is all too easy to be done. '*The ancient proceleusmatick song*' and '*succedaneous means*' are not words which are in everyday speech. And as for the superfluous, we are told of a building 'not destroyed by the tumultuous violence of Knox, but more shamefully suffered to dilapidate by deliberate robbery and frigid indifference.'

Johnson often seems to fail to take his readers sufficiently into consideration. At the beginning of his *Idler* Essay 97 he gave his view that, 'few books disappoint their readers more than the narratives of travellers' and goes on at length to say why. That was in February 1760, but thirteen years later and when he had travelled no further than Durham he was still telling Mrs Thrale, 'You have often heard me complain of finding myself disappointed by books of travels; I am afraid travel itself will end likewise in disappointment.' And sadly we are too often disappointed, as when we are simply told that Dundee is, 'a dirty despicable town'. And there is surely more to be said about Loch Ness than that, 'though not twelve miles broad, it is a very remarkable diffusion of water without islands.' We want to see; to be shown something. We want details, but we are not given them. It is all so reminiscent of Imlac's assertion in *Rasselas*.

> The business of a poet is to examine not the individual but the species; to remark general properties and the large appearances; he does not number the streaks of the tulip or describe the different shades of the forest.

Johnson is an investigator, a reporter, a conveyor of facts. There is very little imagination or evidence of feeling, and almost no trace of empathy with the places he finds himself in, nor with the people he meets. If something does not interest him personally, he ignores it. It is all so different in Boswell's *Journal*. Johnson is at the centre of it as the title page declares, but Boswell has an eye and an ear for everything. This difference is evident from the beginning. In Johnson's second paragraph we are told that Edinburgh is, 'a city too well known to admit description.' And that's that, though they were there for three days. Turning to Boswell we learn that on one occasion, 'He [Johnson] asked to have his lemonade made sweeter; upon which the waiter, with his greasy fingers, lifted a lump of sugar and put it into it. The Doctor, in indignation, threw it out of the window.' The window was, seemingly, open. And recalling that, 'walking the streets of Edinburgh at night was pretty perilous and a good deal odoriferous', he tells us that Johnson 'grumbled in my ear "I smell you in the dark."' Observations like this are what stay in our minds and are the lifeblood of a work. Johnson is all too often anaemic.

During their time in Edinburgh Johnson was introduced to, and met up with, so many different people; and all this Boswell records, together with the conversations they had. It amounts to a total of twenty pages and in this respect his *Journal* could be said to be a rehearsal or dry-run for all those verbatim accounts in the extended *Life* which was to follow six years later. It therefore raises the perennial and unanswerable question of how such a thing could possibly have been achieved. How did he record all these extended and intellectual conversations: with their rumble and flow, the logic of their arguments, the exotic vocabulary coupled with such precision of syntax? That he did it in London is astonishing enough, but travelling across Scotland and for three months? Did he have the most prodigious memory? Did he have quill pens, ink and quantities of paper about him at all times? Or did he have an average memory, coupled with an active imagination and the skills and gifts of a dramatist? There is no answer, but whatever the truth, we have, as a result, two pieces of literature we would not wish to be without.

Reading Johnson, however, we do repeatedly ask ourselves: did he really know what readers of travel books wanted? On 13 September Boswell wrote, 'We were resolved to pay a visit at Kingsburgh and see the celebrated Miss Flora Macdonald.' *Celebrated* she certainly was; a romantic figure and possibly the most famous woman in the whole of Scotland, yet all we learn from Johnson is that, 'She is a woman of middle stature, soft features, gentle manners and elegant presence.' A description which would have fitted several hundred other Scottish ladies at the very least. That evening she told them how she had helped 'Bonnie Prince Charlie', disguised as her maid, to escape to Skye, Johnson did remark to Boswell, 'All this should be written down', but made no attempt to do so himself. Boswell, to his great credit, followed the advice and did write at length of their visit and the account of the escapade Flora had given them. The saddest thing we learn is that after Flora had risked her life to save him, the Prince showed her no gratitude whatsoever, though she could have earned herself the astonishing amount of £30,000 by betraying him. Instead she and her husband became so poor as a result of the Highland Clearances that in 1774, the year after Johnson's visit, they emigrated to America, only to return before long to Skye and a life of hardship, while the 'Bonnie' Prince lived a life of idleness, corpulence and drink in the sophisticated elegance of Rome.

This is not the only disappointment in Johnson's book. One might have expected some emotional, even spiritual response to the island of Iona, which he describes as, 'That illustrious island which was once the luminary of the Celtic region, whence savage clans and roving barbarians derived the benefits of knowledge and the blessings of religion.' He goes on, 'To abstract the mind from all local emotion would be impossible, if it were endeavoured, and would be foolish, if it were possible.' But it would seem that it is possible, at least it was for Samuel Johnson. He says that he, 'surveyed the place' and indeed his language is that of a surveyor. He points out the difference between the Roman and Gothic arches of the episcopal church; makes 'rude measures' and concludes that 'the tower is firm and wants only to be floored and covered.' There is more of the same and when the time comes for them to leave we are told, 'We now left these illustrious ruins by which Mr Boswell was much affected, nor would I willingly be thought to have looked upon them without some emotion.' But there is no written evidence of any such emotion. It is as though to display emotion would be to stoop, and 'I choose not to stoop', as Browning's count once said.

Johnson stands on his dignity and fails to relate to people, as Boswell recognised, 'I regretted that Dr Johnson did not practise the art of accommodating himself to different sorts of people.' When writing of the people of Skye it is as though he regards them as a separate species, such is his detachment. 'Having little work to do, they are not willing, nor perhaps able to endure a long continuance of manual labour, and are therefore considered as habitually idle.'

Johnson had once observed to Boswell that, 'books of travels will be good in proportion to what a man has previously in his mind.' And he certainly took his prejudices with him. It is all very well Boswell saying that, 'He had no ill-will to the Scotch', many of his fellow countrymen did take exception to remarks such as, 'Till the Union made then acquainted with English manners, the culture of their lands was unskilful, and their domestic life unformed; their tables were coarse as the feasts of Esquimaux and their houses as filthy as the cottages of Hottentots.'

Johnson's chief strength was as a gatherer of facts, a reporter, and the rain and high winds that detained them on Skye allowed him to write what he was best at: an essay. For that is what his 17,000-word entry under the heading *Ostig in Sky* amounts to.

Given a number and included among the *Rambler* papers, it would not be seen as an interloper. It is an impressive performance and it would be hard to point to any aspect of Hebridean life he has not covered, such is the range and breadth of the topics. He writes on the geology and climate, the economics, industrial potential and agriculture, the social structure, folklore and food, even instances of second sight.

Interestingly, although they passed close to the site of the Battle of Culloden, there was only a passing reference made to it by Boswell, and none at all by Johnson. Perhaps they realised that anything they said would be sure to upset somebody and yet on Skye Johnson wrote perceptively and with some degree of sensitivity of its consequences. He recognised that the disarming of the clans had caused resentment among those who had been loyal and fought for the King. He also observed that chiefs and lairds, deprived of some of their ancient rights and privileges, had in consequence raised their rents and that this was the factor behind the debilitating increase in emigration; at this point the book ceases to be a travelogue and it becomes polemic:

> Some method to stop this epidemic desire of wandering which spreads its contagion from valley to valley, deserves to be sought with great diligence. In more fruitful countries, the removal of one only makes a room for the succession of another; but in the Hebrides the loss of an inhabitant leaves a lasting vacuity; for nobody born in another part of the world will choose this country for his residence.

There was one other issue which raised Johnson's hackles and that was *Ossian*. In 1760 the Scottish poet James Macpherson had published *Fingal*, supposedly a translation of the poems of an ancient Gaelic poet *Ossian.* They were an instant success, but doubts soon arose as to their authenticity. Johnson was quick to denounce Macpherson as 'a mountebank, a liar and a fraud'. When challenged to produce the originals Macpherson simply refused. When the topic was raised on Skye, Johnson had a quick response, 'to revenge reasonable incredulity, by refusing evidence, is a degree of insolence with which the world is not yet acquainted; and stubborn audacity is the last refuge of guilt.'

It was mid-October before the weather relented and they were able to leave Skye and return to the mainland. After calling in at Col, Iona and Mull they landed at Oban and made their way south to Glasgow which warranted no more notice from Johnson than Edinburgh had. 'To describe a city so much visited as Glasgow is unnecessary,' he declared, yet he had been to neither before.

From there they travelled south again to Auchinlech, 'an estate devolved through a long series of ancestors to Mr Boswell's father.' Boswell had not been looking forward to this as he knew only too well that Johnson and his father differed on so many points and before they arrived he begged Johnson to avoid any reference to Whiggism and Presbyterianism. At first all went well, but looking together through one of the laird's collections, an Oliver Cromwell coin was noticed. Inevitably that led to Charles I and, as Boswell put it, 'They became exceedingly warm and violent.' Poor Boswell. His loyalties were torn. 'It would certainly be very unbecoming in me to exhibit my honoured father, and my respected friend, as intellectual gladiators for the entertainment of the public, and therefore I suppress what would, I dare say, make an interesting scene in this dramatic sketch.' Yes, I dare say it would.

No doubt common courtesy on both sides brought hostilities to an end and the travellers set off for Edinburgh and home. It was 26 November when Johnson arrived back in London; he had been away for almost four months. But his travels were not over. The Thrales were planning to take him on a tour of Wales the following summer and leaving things to the last minute, as usual, he wrote his *Journey to the Western Islands of Scotland*, we are told, in 20 days, finishing it just before they left in June. Various printing hold-ups, however, meant that it was not published until the following January. It met with a somewhat mixed reception, especially among its Scottish readers. Boswell refers to, 'miserable cavillings' in the press and Johnson responded grumpily, 'No Scotchman publishes a book, but there are five hundred ready to applaud him.' And on learning that sales were not good he said he found it strange, 'for in that book I have told the world a great deal that it did not know before.' That is true, but whereas it was strong on enlightenment, (Horace's dictum was: *aut prodesse ... aut delectare*) it was less so on delight.

With an astute sense of timing, Boswell waited until 1785, the year after Johnson's death, before publishing his *Journal of a Tour of the Hebrides*, and as it is more about Johnson than it is about Scotland, its success was immediately guaranteed. The two books are so very different: one stolid and factual, a public performance; the other lively, personal and anecdotal. They complement each other so perfectly one could wish that the two travellers might have collaborated on a single publication. Of course the very idea of Johnson agreeing to collaborate with anyone is quite unthinkable. But if we did, for one moment, allow ourselves to entertain such a thought, what a book we would have before us.

7
THE EDITOR

WITH ONLY FOUR PENCE BETWEEN THEM in their pockets, and having walked almost all the way from Lichfield, Johnson and Garrick must have looked an unlikely duo when they first arrived in London in March 1737. Apart from the disparity in their ages – Johnson was 28 and Garrick only 20 – Johnson was a big, ungainly man, scarred by scrofula, while young Garrick was small, slim and dapper. No one, seeing them that day, could possibly have imagined that such a pair would between them come to effect major and lasting changes in both Shakespearean theatre and criticism.

Initially this was all down to Garrick. Johnson had published his poem *London* in 1738 and his *Life of Mr Richard Savage* in 1744, but his name had not appeared on either title page and for a short time, as we have seen, he had been reduced to absolute penury. David Garrick, in contrast, had made such a name for himself as an actor that by 1747 he was able to lay out £8000 to take over the management of the Drury Lane Theatre, inviting Johnson to write a Prologue for his opening night.

It cannot have been easy for Johnson to see his sometime pupil become so wealthy and successful. He must have been envious, but while they did fall out from time to time, they remained friends and when Garrick died in 1779 Johnson declared that his death had 'eclipsed the gaiety of nations.'

It was Garrick's performance as Macbeth in 1774 which had so astonished London audiences. Gone was the old rodomontade which had long been in fashion. Instead they were witness to a portrayal of a character which aimed for a far greater degree of naturalism. Johnson had helped Garrick to put together a text for the production but nevertheless told Boswell that, 'He (Garrick) has not made Shakespeare better known. He does not understand him.' And again, 'there was not one of his scene-shifters who could not have spoken *To be or not to be* better than he did.' It was a clear case of the player versus the academic, one who spoke the words and one who read them.

Johnson's response to Garrick's performance came in the following year when he published *Miscellaneous Observations on the Tragedy of Macbeth*. In it we see glimpses of the perceptive literary criticism which was to follow. Among the proposed emendations in his Notes (and there are 46 of them) are some of brilliant simplicity, as

> Up, up and see
> The great doom's visage, Malcolm, Banquo
> As from your graves, rise up

where his suggestion that the comma before the names should be replaced by a full stop. It totally changes the tone.

In contrast he wrote a piece on *Macbeth* in *Rambler* 168 in which we find an example of his obtuseness and how shackled he could still be by Augustan notions of decorum, and how offended he could be by 'low terms'. The offending lines were:

> Come, thick night!
> And pall thee in the dunnest smoke of hell,
> That my keen knife see not the wound it makes;
> Nor heav'n peep through the blanket of the dark
> To cry, Hold! Hold!

The first 'low term' he objects to is *knife*, for 'we do not immediately conceive that any crime of importance is to be committed with a *knife*.' But then, 'I can scarce check my risibility,' he tells us, 'when it comes to blanket. Who without some relaxation of his gravity can hear the avengers of guilt "peep through a blanket?"' The pomposity of Johnson's language here is itself so revealing. It is also worth noting that he attributes the lines to Macbeth, whereas they are actually spoken by Lady Macbeth.

The pamphlet *Miscellaneous Observations* was greeted with well-deserved praise, and printed with it was a separate sheet *Proposal for Printing a New Edition of the Plays of William Shakespeare*. In it, for the first time, were set out the tasks which would ever after face any Shakespearian editor, commentator or critic. What he promises is an edition 'with notes, critical and explanatory, in which the text will be corrected; the various readings remarked; the conjectures of former editors examined and their omissions supplied.' It was a brave endeavour, but it was not to be. The bookseller Jacob Tonson stepped in and claimed that he owned the copyright to Shakespeare. Rather a contentious claim one would have thought, seeing that there had already been four previous editions. Nevertheless, Tonson's claim prevailed and Johnson's proposals were put on hold. But he was not long out of work. In June 1746 he signed the contract for the Dictionary and was kept busy at that until 1755. When it was finished, there followed one of his bouts of melancholia, so that when the Shakespeare scheme was put to him, again his first reaction was, 'I think I will not do it.' An understandable reaction when one thinks of it as being more of the same kind of work – a concentration on minutiae. But he needed money and so agreed.

The *Proposals for Printing the Dramatick Works of William Shakespeare* which he published in 1756 declared a clear objective from the outset. 'The business of him who republishes an ancient book is to correct what is corrupt and explain what is obscure.' And he shows a positive understanding of how the text of this particular 'ancient book' had become so corrupt. It had never been meant to be printed, but was written out for actors and further handwritten copies made time and again as needs arose, inevitably incurring blunders made by hasty and probably ill-educated copyists. And when they were printed, they were done so from compilations of separate parts and sometimes printed surreptitiously by rival groups. As he says, 'It is not easy for invention to bring together so many causes concurring to vitiate a text.'

On the question of obscurity he is equally clear-sighted, aware that language intended for the theatre needs to be understood immediately and so required 'the use of common colloquial language which might therefore have dropped out of usage.' Added to this he states that the plays were written when the language was in a state of fluctuation with new words being adopted from other countries all the time.

His most valuable perception is that, 'very few of his lines were difficult to his audience and that he used expressions therefore as were then common.' Unlike his predecessors, Johnson did not immediately change what he did not understand; he sought an explanation. Added to this he recognised the rapidity of Shakespeare's imagination, 'which might hurry him to a second thought before he had fully explained the first.'

The scheme he proposes for an editor to overcome those two problems was one which had never been attempted before, but which has become standard practice ever since: in effect a variorum edition, elucidating obscurities, tracing references, and proposing emendations based on careful consideration of the language.

The outstanding position Shakespeare occupies in the annals of literature is (*pace* Baconians *et al*) now so beyond question that it comes as something of a surprise that in his 1765 Preface Johnson seems to need to justify the task he is about to undertake. Serious critical and textual attention of this nature was generally looked upon as being the preserve of the ancients, while Shakespeare was not so far short of still being a modern.

His opening gambit is a consideration of Shakespeare's genius in the creation of characters, and this immediately raises an issue of some importance. His characterisation is certainly something for which Shakespeare is famous: Hamlet, Othello, Lear. But there are different ways of looking at it. In the not too distant past, 'character analysis' was a central feature of Shakespearean studies and what it was set on demonstrating was the *individuality* of his creations, and at times they came to be envisaged as so *real* that in extreme cases they were regarded as having an actual existence beyond and outside the text. There was even a book called *The Girlhood of Shakespeare's Heroines.* It was Professor L.C. Knights' ground-breaking essay 'How many children had Lady Macbeth?' which eventually put an end to that.

Such an approach would have horrified Johnson. He agreed totally with the brilliance of the characterisation, but for him the achievement depended on the very fact that they were *not* individuals. Again we hear Imlac's assertion that the poet, 'does not number the streaks of the tulip.' Or, as was put so startlingly by Thomas Rhymer, 'A poet is not to follow his fancy, for then his fancy might be monstrous, might be singular and please nobody's maggot but his own.' Singularity was to be avoided. General principles were what was wanted, for, as Johnson argued, 'Nothing can please many and please long but just representations of general nature.' And that was exactly what he found, and what so pleased him in Shakespeare. In some writers, he said, 'a character is too often an individual; in those of Shakespeare it is commonly a species. It is from this wide extension of design that so much instruction is derived. It is this which fills the plays of Shakespeare with practical axioms and domestic wisdom.' Nothing shows more clearly the difference between our approach to literature and that of Johnson. For him, didacticism was its chief end. It would never occur to us to look for 'domestic wisdom' in *Othello* or *Hamlet*, and the notion that it 'fills the plays' seems to us both monstrous and singular. Even more so is his contention that 'it may be said of Shakespeare that from his works may be collected a system of civil and economic prudence.' Yet it is this attitude which enables him to assert that Shakespeare is not simply writing about, and for, his own time, but for all time, 'accommodating his sentiments to real life' in such a way that 'he has not only shewn human nature as it acts in real exigencies, but as it would be found in trials to which it cannot be exposed.' The conclusions he reaches here are ones we find ourselves in total agreement with.

We are on his side too when he takes issue with 'The censure which he has incurred by mixing comic and tragic scenes.' Dryden had had no time for Shakespeare's puns and quibbles, his 'mean buffoonery, vile ribaldry and unmannerly jests.' Pope tended to be of the same mind, but was more understanding. He recognised that as well as being a writer Shakespeare was also an actor and so understood his audiences, who, he says, were 'generally composed of the meaner sort of people.' But Johnson adopts a far more positive approach by pointing out quite simply that real life is never simple and that consequently Shakespeare's plays are 'neither tragedies nor comedies, but compositions of a distinct kind, exhibiting the real states of sublunary nature, which partakes of good and evil, joy and sorrow.' But what follows is not at all what one expects. 'In tragedy he often writes with great appearance of toil and study, what is written at last with little felicity; but in his comic scenes, he seems to produce without labour, what no labour can improve ... In his tragic scenes there is always something wanting, but his comedy often surpasses expectation or desire ... His tragedy seems to be skill, his comedy to be instinct.' That he should exalt the comedies over the tragedies is simply so eccentric as to be beyond one's understanding. The primacy of tragedy had been a sine qua non since the time of Aristotle.

He seems almost to be aware of this himself when he asserts even of the mixing of the tragic and the comic that while it 'is a practice contrary to the rules of criticism, there is always an appeal open from criticism to nature.' But in his very next sentence he shows that there will be no deviation from one Augustan tenet of belief. 'The end of writing is to instruct; the end of poetry is to instruct by pleasure.'

And Shakespeare is found, in Johnson's view, to be 'more careful to please than instruct.' Evil is not always punished and good is not always rewarded. One need look no further than the death of Cordelia at the end of *King Lear.* 'This fault the barbarity of his age cannot extenuate.' The fault, in Johnson's view, is as obvious as that and there is no arguing about it.

There is no sign whatsoever of *bardolatry* in Johnson's Preface. In some of Shakespeare's 'effusions of passion' he finds 'meanness, tediousness and obscurity'. His narration is 'a wearisome train of circumlocution'. And as for the 'tender emotion', he is 'not long soft and pathetic without some idle conceit or contemptible equivocation ... a quibble is the golden apple for which he will always turn aside.'

At his point we read with some relief that he is about to defend Shakespeare against the charge of not keeping to the dramatic unities of time, place and action. And he does so at some considerable length, but basically arguing that people watching in a theatre know that they are in a theatre and that it is not real. And although he says, 'I am almost frightened of my own temerity' in so claiming, he was actually kicking down a door that was already open and had been for some time. Dryden had done the task for him in his essay 'On Dramatic Poetry' very nearly a hundred years earlier, and Pope had put it acutely, 'To judge therefore of Shakespeare by Aristotle's rules, is like trying a man by the laws of one country, who acted under those of another.' Johnson's tone seems to suggest that it had never crossed anyone's mind before. But he concludes with a splendid image:

> The work of a correct and regular writer is a garden accurately formed and diligently planted, varied with shades and scented with flowers; the composition of Shakespeare is a forest, in which oaks extend their branches, and pines tower in the air, interspersed sometimes with weeds and brambles, and sometimes giving shelter to myrtles and to roses; filling the eye with awful pomp, and gratifying the mind with endless diversity.

The advantage Johnson had over other editors was his Dictionary. The years he had spent working on it had given him experience of the staying-power necessary for so much close attention to minutiae. He had construed precise and extended definitions for over 40,000 words, so that when it was a question of the elucidation of meaning his knowledge was without parallel. Added to these definitions had been the illustrative quotations and Shakespeare comes second only in quantity to the Bible, which suggests that Johnson had read the plays even more often than Garrick.

The extent of his etymology can be seen in what would appear to be the most insignificant of words. A line in *Henry VIII*, 'the many to them longing' is explained, 'The *many* is the *meiny*, the train, the people.' And he then adds, 'Dryden is perhaps the last to use the word' and cites the usage. In *Love's Labour's Lost* when Don Armando calls Moth 'dear imp' we are told that '*Imp* was anciently a term of dignity' with the added and delightful piece of information that 'Lord Cromwell in his last letter to Henry VIII prays for "the imp his son".' And there are occasions when

Johnson shows how his own learning outdoes Shakespeare's. In *A Midsummer Night's Dream* a mention of 'the fiery glow-worm's eyes' is challenged. 'I know not how Shakespeare, who commonly derived his knowledge of nature from his own observation, happened to place the glow-worm's light in his eyes, which is only in his tail.' But Johnson is wrong too: it is the female which glows.

At the end of each play comes a section in which Johnson outlines his thoughts and reactions. For the most part they are brief and generalised, but the major tragedies did occasion some interesting essays, especially *King Lear*. What is remarkable is that during the whole of the eighteenth century no one ever saw a performance of Shakespeare's play. What they saw was Nahum Tate's sanitised version written in 1681 in which neither Lear nor Cordelia die. He regains his throne and she marries Edgar, who proclaims finally and triumphantly that, 'truth and virtue shall at last succeed.' Nothing to upset anybody. Johnson was of course obliged to print Shakespeare's full text, but could hardly bring himself to read it as he did so. 'I might relate that I was many years ago so shocked by Cordelia's death that I know not whether I ever endured to read again the last scenes of the play till I undertook to revise them as an editor.' He was firmly of the opinion that an audience would 'always rise better pleased from the final triumph of virtue.'

Nevertheless there are among these notes and brief essays some pointers to the criticism which was soon to follow in his *Lives of the English Poets*.

8

THE LIVES OF THE ENGLISH POETS

IN MARCH 1777 JOHNSON MET UP with the representatives of a consortium of 40 London publishers and agreed on a fee of 200 Guineas to provide them with prefaces to each of the poets in an anthology they were planning. When telling Boswell of it he said, 'I am engaged to write little lives, and little prefaces to a little anthology of the English poets.' But he cannot have been paying attention when he agreed to the proposal. It was far from being little. There would be 52 poets and it took him four years to complete. Equally the editors cannot have expected what they got for their money. A few of the prefaces are brief, but most are not and some amount to book-length assessments. The biographical section alone on Alexander Pope amounts to 37,000 words.

First in the list comes Abraham Cowley, a poet of some distinction in his own day, but now largely forgotten. Johnson considered this essay 'the best of the whole', according to Boswell, 'on account of the dissertation which it contains on the Metaphysical Poets.' It is a dissertation which has had a mixed history. Originally it was seen as a splendid attack on what were regarded as the extremes and follies of those poets, but when their reputations were in the ascendency again, particularly in the twentieth century, Johnson's views were looked on as a narrow-minded failure to appreciate what was different.

But perhaps neither view is right. When Johnson wrote, 'The most heterogeneous ideas were yoked by violence together; nature and art ransacked for illustrations, comparisons and allusions', he is showing a very positive understanding, if not appreciation, of what were their outstanding characteristics. And his subsequent observations are not altogether a condemnation. 'To write on their plan, it was at least necessary to read and think.' In this he was reacting against a fashion for vacuous lyricism, but at the same time objecting on the grounds of his basic critical tenet, namely that, 'Great thoughts are always general and consist in positions not limited by exceptions, and in descriptions not descending to minuteness.' The word to notice here is *descending*.

Johnson had once told Boswell that, 'When I was a young fellow I wanted to write a Life of Dryden.' And his opening words here show that he is now happily on home ground. 'Of the great poet whose life I am about to delineate ... ' But this is to be no hagiography. Very early he declares, 'I wish that there was no necessity of following the progress of his theatrical fame.' Nevertheless, he does so, and at some length. Often, we are told, Dryden, 'accompanied his work with a preface of criticism, a kind of learning then almost new in the English language.' Famously continuing, 'Dryden may be properly considered the father of English criticism.' And what makes his views stand out, he says, is that 'the criticism of Dryden is the criticism of a poet.' But this assertion is never supported by any particular instances; what he gives us is an overview. 'In his general precepts which depend upon the nature of things and the structure of the human mind he may be safely recommended to the confidence of the reader', and then promptly and characteristically adds, 'but his occasional and particular positions were sometimes interested [*biased*] sometimes negligent and sometimes capricious.'

When, at last, he comes to the 'veneration' accorded to Dryden's poetry, it is due, we are told, 'as he refined the language, improved the sentiments and tuned the numbers of English poetry.' Waller and Denham are given token credit for rescuing poetry from 'half a century of forced thought and rugged metre', but Dryden is the acknowledged driving force. After him 'it is apparent English poetry had no tendency to relapse to its former savageness.'

It is soon clear that what Dryden is to be chiefly praised for is his language – the words he chooses and how he uses them – but far less consideration is given to what he uses them *for*. Citing the variations of language which there are: 'scholastic and popular, grave and familiar, elegant and gross', he insists that 'Words too familiar or too remote defeat the purpose of the poet.' He takes it as given that the language of prose is different from that of poetry and that before Dryden there was 'no poetical diction'.

Style interests Johnson more than content and we remember Boswell recording in the early pages of the *Life* that 'He told that from his earliest years he loved to read poetry, but hardly ever read any poem to the end.' So, although from this point on the essay abounds in quotation, what we do not get is any close reading, no exposition or moments of insight such as we have come to expect in the wake of such critics as I.A. Richards, Empson or Leavis. Johnson's is a prescriptive criticism; he likes to lay down laws and then point out infringements of them. He rebukes Dryden for 'forced conceits' in his early work and the improper use of mythology. He even has the self-assurance to argue that, 'The poem concludes with a simile that might have better been omitted.' He is even prepared to go as far as to say, 'It would not be hard to believe that Dryden had written the first two lines seriously and that some wag had had added the two latter in burlesque.' The religious debate in 'The Hind and the Panther', which Swift thought a masterpiece, 'is injudicious and incommodious: for what can be more absurd than that one beast should counsel another to rest her faith upon a pope and council.' So obtusely literal-minded, so lacking in imagination. And this of a poet whom he 'venerates'. But veneration is not the same as handing out praise and there is little of that. 'Absalom and Achitophel', Dryden's most outstanding work, will be 'found to comprise all the excellences of which the subject is susceptible.'

And yet in his final paragraph he again restates his opening contention, 'To him we owe the improvement, perhaps the completion of our metre, the refinement of our language and much of the correctness of our sentiments.' Adding, 'By him we were taught to think naturally and express forcibly.' And finally adapting to English poetry what was said of Augustus' achievement in Rome, he declares, 'he found it brick and left it marble.' Marble, however, is notoriously cold.

While Johnson considered Dryden to be sometimes biased in his criticism, there is no question as to the virulence of his own Tory bias when it came to an assessment of Milton, who had been Latin Secretary to Oliver Cromwell and a leading political figure, still writing in favour of regicide when Charles II had returned to England and was about to take the throne. 'His political notions were those of an acrimonious and surly republicanism ... a republicanism founded in an excess of hatred of greatness, and a sullen desire of independence; in petulance impatient of control and pride disdainful of superiority. He hated monarchs in the state and prelates in the church, for he hated all whom he was required to obey.' And his hostility was not confined to his politics; it included Milton's personal life. 'In domestic relations he was severe and arbitrary [showing] a Turkish contempt for females as subordinate and inferior beings.'

It comes as no great surprise therefore to see this hostility carried over into the criticism. Milton's magnificent sonnets are barely glanced at, while 'Lycidas', regarded by Harold Bloom as the greatest lyric in the English language, is totally shredded.

> In this poem there is no nature, for there is no truth; there is no art, for there is nothing new. Its form is that of a pastoral ... whatever images it can supply are long ago exhausted and its inherent improbability always forces dissatisfaction on the mind ... With these trifling fictions are mingled the most awful and sacred truths, such as ought never to be polluted with such irreverent combinations.

What he fails to recognise is that although 'Lycidas' begins as a pastoral, it very soon becomes an attack on the corruption Milton saw in the established church. Johnson's reading is so wrongheaded one wonders whether this was another of the poems he never managed to read to the end.

Johnson's response to *Paradise Lost* is so complex and so fascinating that debate about it has never ceased. His acceptance of its greatness seems to have needed to be dragged out of him.

George Watson in his book *The Literary Critics* puts it perfectly when he says that Johnson, 'writes about it as though it were a visit to the dentist.'

One of the problems for us is that we can never read *Paradise Lost* in the same way that Johnson read it, and it is not simply that we are separated by a gulf of time, but equally by one of culture and especially of religious belief. We read it as a myth or fable, in the same way that we read *The Odyssey*. For Johnson the *story* was not a story; it was history, sacred fact and he clearly meant it when he said, ' ... in the description of heaven and hell we are all interested, as we are all to reside hereafter either in the regions of horror of bliss.' The literalism of this stops us with quite a jolt.

His opening gambit is familiar, but not one which instantly springs to *our* minds. 'Epic poetry undertakes to teach the most important truths by the most pleasing precepts and therefore relates some great events in the most affecting manner.' He acknowledges that the war in heaven and the fall of man are certainly great events; that 'the characteristic quality of his poem is sublimity'; and that 'every line breathes sanctity of thought.' But does it teach? The truths it contains, he says, are not new, and so, 'what we knew before, we cannot learn.'

The criticisms then begin to mount. 'The good and evil of Eternity are too ponderous for the wings of wit, the mind sinks under them in passive helplessness.' Sometimes his carping descends to a level of silliness, as when he wonders how Satan managed to take his spear and shield with him when he entered the body of the toad!

His chief complaint, however, is that:

> The plan of *Paradise Lost* has this inconvenience, that it comprises neither human actions nor human manners. The man and woman who act and suffer are in a state which no other man or woman can ever know. The reader finds no transaction in which he can be engaged, beholds no condition in which he can by any effort of imagination place himself; he has, therefore, little natural curiosity or sympathy.

This being so, he claims, we cannot learn from it. But the failure of imagination is entirely his. For us, the dilemma faced by Adam and Eve in Book X is all too human. We can easily identify with the *situation* of marital dispute, temptation and guilt and see the presentation itself as an allegory. Yet the allegory is what Johnson found 'unskilful'.

The *coup de grâce* he delivers is swift and deadly.

> The want of human interest is always felt. *Paradise Lost* is one of the books which the reader admires and lays down, and forgets to take up again. No one ever wished it longer than it is. Its perusal is a duty rather than a pleasure.

But this generalisation is simply not true. Many readers – myself being one – have read and re-read it and have felt each time that silence of catharsis which follows those chilling closing lines

> They hand in hand with wandering steps and slow,
> Through Eden took their solitary way.

Lines which remind us that when Milton composed this great work, he was blind and reliant on touch.

It is hard to believe, but I think Johnson would for once have been speechless at Arnold's contention that Pope and Dryden were classics not of poetry but of prose. As he says among his closing comments, 'If Pope be not a poet, where is poetry to be found?' The longest section of his *Life of Pope* is the biographical section. It is masterly, but does concentrate rather too much on the less attractive sides of his nature. No one has ever suggested that Pope was a warm-hearted, loveable being, but Johnson spares him nothing. He even begins, 'The person of Pope is well known not to have been formed by the nicest model', and then goes on, 'the indulgence and accommodation which his sickness required had taught him all the unpleasing and unsocial qualities of a valetudinarian man.' But it was surely going too far when he claims, 'His weakness made it very difficult for him to be clean.'

He was generous in his account of Pope's works. *The Rape of the Lock* is 'the most ingenious and the most delightful of all his compositions.' And of the 'Essay on Criticism' he says, 'If he had written nothing else, it would have placed him among the first critics and the first poets.' Again, however, his observations rarely descend from the general to the particular and when they do they can be very surprising, as when he suggests that the card game in the *Rape of the Lock* 'might be spared.' Yet it is one of the poem's great triumphs; so detailed that the entire game can be played out by the reader, who is also intrigued to have it pointed out that the King of Clubs 'Of all monarchs only grasps the globe' and that the King of Diamonds 'shows but half his face.'

Praise, as with Dryden, is primarily given to technique. Content, when noticed at all, can come in for some harsh words. The 'Essay on Man' is blasted, 'Never was penury of knowledge and vulgarity of sentiment so happily disguised.' And this of a poet he admired. Others get even rougher treatment. Of William Shenstone, a minor but certainly an accomplished poet, we are told, 'his diction is often harsh, improper and affected; his words ill-coined or ill-chosen and his phrases unskilfully invented.'

Most notorious is his treatment of Thomas Gray. He could not abide the man personally, telling Boswell, 'He was dull in company, dull in his closet, dull everywhere. He was dull in a new way and that made many people think he was great.' His mean-spiritedness is evident in his approach to Gray's 'Prospect of Eton College' of which he wrote, 'His supplication to Father Thames to tell him who drives the hoop or tosses the ball is useless and puerile. Father Thames has no better means of knowing than himself.' Who is being puerile here?

And when he turns to Gray's 'Progress of Poetry' his disdain borders on the personally offensive, 'the second stanza is unworthy of notice. Criticism disdains to chase a schoolboy to his commonplaces.' Gray's was a new poetry and Johnson was digging his heels in. The 'Elegy Written in a Country Churchyard' has since been recognised as a major work and one of the best-loved poems in our language, but Johnson is only prepared to go so far as to say, 'Had Gray written often thus, it had been vain to blame and useless to praise him.'

As its full title indicates, the work was intended to include the lives of *English* poets only, but Johnson himself decided that he wanted to include a foreigner – a Scotsman, James Thomson. This is something of a surprise as six years previously in a conversation with Mr Shiels, one of his amanuenses, he had asserted that Thomson's fault was 'such a cloud of words sometimes that the sense can hardly peep through.' And went on to prove it by reading out a passage which, when it had earned Shiels' admiration, he announced, 'Well, Sir, I have omitted every other line.' And yet when he came to write about him, it was with almost unqualified praise, even for his blank verse, a form which rarely met with his approval. 'As a writer,' he declared, 'he is entitled to one praise of the highest kind: his mode of thinking and of expressing his thoughts is original ... he looks round on Nature and on Life with the eye which Nature bestows only on a poet ... The reader of *The Seasons* wonders that he never saw before what Thomson shews him, and that he never yet has felt what Thomson impresses.' James Thomson is a poet whose reputation does not deserve to have slipped so.

Also surprising is Johnson's decision to include Isaac Watts. Equally surprising is that what he is known for today is what Johnson has no time for.

> His ear was well-tuned and his diction was elegant and copious. But his devotional poetry is, like that of others, unsatisfactory. The paucity of its topics enforces perpetual repetition, and the sanctity of the matter rejects the ornament of figurative diction. It is sufficient for Watts to have done better than others what no man has done well.

It is an astonishing assertion and suggests that Johnson had never read George Herbert or Christopher Smart.

In the two and a half centuries since the *Lives* was published, there has been a multitude of editions and it is perhaps not immediately obvious why. We do not go to these essays for instruction, to have something explained to us, or that our taste in literature might be enlarged. We go to them to see what Johnson *thought*, and yet his thinking, his attitude was already looking out of date. As Lytton Strachey put it, 'He judged authors as though they were criminals in the dock, answering for any infraction of the rules and regulations laid down by the laws of art, which it was his business to administer.' The music and the flights of fancy to be found in poetry counted for nothing with Johnson. He seemed to have no ear and no imagination.

His judgements and pronouncements are, however, invariably interesting, even if frequently wrong. He was wrong about Milton, wrong about Donne and wrong about Gray. But he was often wrong in such an interesting way. Once read, his verdict on 'Lycidas', 'easy, vulgar and therefore disgusting' (changed though the meanings of those three words are) is not likely to be forgotten. And some of his perceptions are brilliantly precise, as of *The Rape of the Lock* where he points out that 'New things are made familiar and familiar things new.'

'As one reads, the brilliant sentences seem to come to us, out of the past, with the friendliness of a conversation.' This wise observation again comes from an essay by Lytton Strachey, whose witty and elegant critical essays also deserve to be read, and on the very same grounds.

The *Lives* was Johnson's last substantial work and when the final volumes were published in 1781 he had only a few years left to live and they were not happy ones. He fell out with his great friend Mrs Thrale – she had not only married beneath her, but an Italian – and that good old man Dr Levet died.

In June 1783 Johnson had a stroke which temporarily deprived him of the power of speech, a particularly unkind blow, yet he was still able to revise the *Lives* for a new edition. But he knew his end was near. He wrote a will leaving a substantial legacy to his black servant Francis Barber, and, great correspondent that he had been, told Boswell that a sad thought had struck him, 'We shall receive no letters in the grave.'

Nevertheless, he still had it in him to write one more poem. His boyhood version of Horace's *Ode II xiv* had insisted on the inevitability of death and here in *Ode IV vii* he returns to that same theme. It is an elegant, disciplined and carefully crafted poem, as this extract shows. It is a free translation, with the casual colloquialism of the word 'toss' in the final line being particularly brilliant. As we read it, however, we recognise it as being, sadly, an elegy for himself.

> The changing year's successive plan
> Proclaims mortality to man.
> Rough winter's blasts to spring give way,
> Spring yields to summer's sovereign ray,
> Then summer sinks in autumn's reign
> And winter chills the world again.
> Her losses soon the moon supplies
> But wretched man, when once he lies
> Where Priam and his sons are laid
> Is naught but ashes and a shade.
> Who knows if Jove who counts our score
> Will toss us in a morning more?

He died on the evening of 13 December 1784 at the age of 75 and was buried in Westminster Abbey. The world of literature, as one memorialist put it, 'was perplexed and distressed – as a swarm of bees that have lost their queen.'

BIBLIOGRAPHY

Walter Jackson Bate, *The Achievement of Samuel Johnson* (Oxford, 1955)

Walter Jackson Bate, *Samuel Johnson* (New York, 1977)

Neil Curry, *Six Eighteenth-century Poets* (London, 2011)

David Crystal, ed. *Samuel Johnson: A Dictionary of the English Language* (London, 2005)

Ian Finlayson, *The Moth and the Candle* (London, 1984)

Donald Greene, *Samuel Johnson* (Boston, 1989)

Jean H. Hagstrum, *Samuel Johnson's Literary Criticism* (Chicago, 1967)

J.P. Hardy, *Samuel Johnson: A Critical Study* (London, 1979)

Henry Hitchings, *Dr Johnson's Dictionary* (London, 2005)

Richard Holmes, *Dr Johnson & Mr Savage* (London, 1993)

Richard Holmes, *Johnson on Savage* (London, 2005)

Mary Hyde, *The Impossible Friendship* (London, 1973)

Lawrence Lipking, *Johnson: The Life of an Author* (Harvard, 1998)

David Littlejohn, *Dr Johnson: His Life in Letters* (New Jersey, 1965)

David Nokes, *Samuel Johnson: A Life* (London, 2009)

Bruce Redford, *The Converse of the Pen* (Chicago, 1986)

Pat Rogers, *Samuel Johnson* (London, 1993)

Pat Rogers, *Johnson & Boswell in Scotland* (London, 1993)

Adam Sisman, *Boswell's Presumptuous Task* (New York, 2001)

Lytton Strachey, *Books and Characters* (London, 1922)

David Nichol Smith, *Shakespeare in the Eighteenth Century* (London, 1928)

David Venturo, *Johnson the Poet* (London, 1999)

George Watson, *The Literary Critics* (London, 1986)

W.K. Wimsatt, *Dr Johnson on Shakespeare* (London, 1960)

INDEX

Addison, Joseph 50, 61, 66
Arnold, Matthew 124
Auchinloch, Lord 106

Bailey, Nathan 50
Barber, Frank 83, 128
Beckett, Samuel 96
Blake, William 88
Bloom, Harold 122
Boswell, James 13-15, 18, 23, 53, 55, 59, 70, 74, 77, 79, 97-99, 101-108, 118-120, 126, 128

Charles Stuart, *Bonnie Prince* 103
Chesterfield, Lord 56-58
Coleridge, S.T. 58
Cowley, Abraham 118
Cowper, William 44

Defoe, Daniel 17
Denham, John 120
Dodsley, Robert 50-51, 56
Donne, John 49, 128

Dryden, John 26, 49, 54, 61, 114-116, 118-121, 124
Duck, Stephen 22

Empson, William 120

Fielding, Henry 17, 71

Garrick, David 14, 32, 34, 55, 108, 109, 116
Gentleman's Magazine 16, 46, 57, 58
Gray, Thomas 126-128

Hawkins, Sir John 18
Herbert, George 127
Hicks, William 83
Hobbes, Thomas 62
Horace 27, 128

Johnson, Elizabeth (Tetty) 14, 64-65, 67

Johnson, Samuel
Works
  The Adventurer 65, 72, 75-76, 88

Dictionary 15, 25, 38, 49-63, 64, 86, 111, 118
The Idler 65, 76-81, 86, 100
Irene 32-36, 73
A Journey to the Western Islands of Scotland 97-107
The Lives of the English Poets 15, 25, 117-128
London 15, 19, 26-32, 43, 51, 108
Prologue for Drury Lane 33-34, 115
The Rambler 18, 20, 24, 34, 38, 56, 63, 65-75, 77, 78, 86, 91, 105, 109
Rasselas 15, 38, 81-96
Shakespeare 62, 108-117
The Vanity of Human Wishes 15, 37-43, 45, 56, 66, 73, 87, 94
Universal Chronicle 76, 80

Johnson, Sarah 82

Jonson, Ben 33

Juvenal, 26-28, 30, 38, 42

Knights, L.C. 113

Leavis, F.R. 120

Lobo, Jerome
  A Voyage to Abyssinia 81, 82
Levet, Robert 45-48, 83, 128

Macaulay, Thomas 74

Macdonald, Flora 102-103

Macpherson, James 105-106

Milton, John 25, 48, 54, 120-124, 128

Mondboddo, Lord 100

Montagu, Elizabeth 66

Murray, Arthur 45

Newbery, John 76-77

Ossian 105

Percy, Thomas 34, 54, 55

Pope, Alexander 19, 25, 27, 50, 54, 61, 68, 114, 118, 124-125

Reynolds, Joshua 82

Rhymer, Thomas 113

Richards, I.A. 120

Richardson, Samuel 24

Rogers, Samuel 66

Savage, Richard 16-20, 26, 51, 72, 108

Shaftesbury, Lord 62

Shakespeare, William 54, 61, 76, 108-117

Shenstone, William 125-126

Smart, Christopher 127

Strachey, Lytton 127-128

Steele, Richard 19, 66

Swift, Jonathan *42, 121*

Tate, Nahum *117*
Thrale, Hester *36, 62, 99, 100, 128*
Thomson, James *22, 126-127*
Tonson, Jacob *117*

Waller, Edmund *120*
Walpole, Robert *29-30*
Watts, Isaac *127*
Watson, George *123*
Wordsworth, William *100*